GW00724946

The *CHAMPAGNE* *ALMANAC*

DON PHILPOTT

ERIC DOBBY PUBLISHING

Published by Eric Dobby Publishing Ltd.,
12 Warnford Road, Orpington, Kent BR6 6LW.

A catalogue record for this book is available from the British Library
ISBN 1-85882-007-13
Typeset in 8.5 pt on 9 pt by Origination, Luton
Printed and bound in Great Britain by
BPCC Hazell Books Ltd
Member of BPCC Ltd

CONTENTS

INTRODUCTION

Noel Coward was asked one day why he drank
Champagne for breakfast. 'Doesn't everyone?' he
replied.

Champagne is the Wine of Kings, and the King of
Wines.

If imitation is the sincerest form of flattery then
Champagne has admirers all round the world. There
are many excellent sparkling wines produced
nowadays, but there is only one Champagne, and it is
still the undisputed champion in the sparkling wine
league. It has been copied in all the major wine-
producing regions of the world and although there is a
growing number of pretenders to the throne,
Champagne has never been truly equalled.

It is fair to say, however, that Champagne has gone
through a troubled patch over the past couple of years,
with the collapse of the traditional agreement between
growers and the Champagne Houses, and the effects
of rising retail prices in a world hit by recession. A
three-year deal has been agreed between the growers
and the Champagne Houses, and it is likely that this
will become the basis for a more permanent contract
which will bring stability to the market.

The other major problem is that there is just not
enough Champagne to go round. Production is limited,
while demand continues to grow worldwide. In 1945
less than 22 million bottles of Champagne were
available for the home and export market while by the
end of 1992 production was the equivalent of 280
million bottles.

The last two years have seen steadily rising retail
prices and a shake-up of traditional markets. The
severe spring frosts in 1991 caused serious damage to
many Champagne vineyards although those that
escaped reported slightly larger than average yields at
the *vendange*. The 1991 harvest produced 278 million
bottles, and the 1992 was the fourth largest yield on
record at 280 million bottles, although almost a
quarter of the 'must' has been put in reserve to

supplement any shortfall in future years.

In 1992 growers reached agreement before the harvest to reduce the price of grapes below the 1991 level, which helped stabilise the price of Champagne. And, in 1992 a number of new measures were introduced designed to further enhance quality and stability.

These included limiting yield per hectare to 10,400 kilos per hectare, although individual growers can apply for supplementary yield, controlling the quality of grapes pressed – 160 kilos per hectare which effectively abolishes the 'deuxième taille' – and even more rigorous selection of grapes during harvesting by hand.

There are signs that the recession in Europe and the United States has bottomed out. The decline in Champagne sales caused by recession, the Gulf War and higher prices, which was felt throughout most of 1991 coupled with depressed markets for much of 1992, appears to have halted and all the signs are that Champagne sales are rising again. There is no doubt that Champagne will face increasing competition from other sparklers in different parts of the world, but its position as the King of Wines is assured.

CHAMPAGNE
The Area

Champagne is the most northerly vineyard area of
France, and the word *champagne* comes from the Latin
word for a plain. The province is really one large plain,
145 km (90 miles) or so to the north-east of Paris, and
the vines are grown on the gently-sloping hills which
break up the landscape. The whole area was formerly
the basin of a huge inland sea, and as the marine life
died and fell to the seabed, a thick layer of nutrient-rich
chalk was built up. This is now the soil of Champagne
and one of the main reasons for its very special
qualities. The region is split by the River Marne which
runs from east to west through wooded hills composed
mainly of clay soils. In the river valley is to be found
Epernay, the Champagne town, while on the plains is
Reims, the Champagne capital.

The average annual temperature in Champagne is
10°C (50°F), about the lowest temperature at which
vines can flourish, but the slight elevation of the
vineyards on the gentle slopes protects them from all but
the most severe spring frosts, when the worst damage
can be done because the sap is rising. The chalk soil not
only retains the heat of the sun which warms the roots
and reflects the sun's rays; it also keeps the soil well
drained, and the nearby forests and woodlands help to
regulate the humidity of the region. The chalk extends
for many metres below ground, and it is not only
suitable for vines; it has allowed the growers to carve
out perfect cellars, and there are now more than 160
kilometres of tunnels and caves in the chalk.

Vines have certainly flourished in Champagne since
Roman times. In 57BC Julius Caesar found himself in
Champagne, having conquered Gaul. A Belgic tribe, the
Rémois, were already established in the province and
they offered the emperor their allegiance. In gratitude,
Julius ordered the building of a town, Durocortorum,
'the Capital of the Second Belgium', where eight major
routes met. The town survived for nearly 500 years as a
show-place, with its statues and theatres.

In AD92 the Emperor Domitian ordered the uprooting of half the vineyards in the Empire so that more land could be made available for growing grain. Vines were only to be grown in areas near large military camps, so that wine could be produced for the soldiers. Champagne was one of the areas ordered to destroy its vineyards, but the edict from Rome was ignored by some growers. Wine has, therefore, been produced in Champagne almost continuously for some 2,000 years.

Reims has suffered through the centuries because of its situation in the north-east of France, close to the border. In the fifth century, when the Roman Empire was in decline and troops were withdrawn from Gaul, Reims was exposed to attack. The first invader was Attila the Hun. Reims was sacked and set on fire, as were the much smaller towns of Epernay and Châlons. The powerful Archbishop of Reims managed to rally the inhabitants and restore order. Indeed, so powerful were they that it was Archbishop St. Rémi who baptised Clovis as the first Frankish king in Reims Cathedral in 496. Reims, incidentally, is not named after St. Rémi, but after the Rémois. It was the Archbishop's coronation of Clovis which established the links between the city and the monarchy, and made his church the national cathedral.

Because of their links with royalty through Reims, the nobility of the province exercised immense power and influence at the French court. The Duke of Reims ruled his territory as a king, and the Count of Châlons was also the bishop of the diocese, commanding both spiritual and temporal loyalty.

Great religious institutions, such as the abbeys of S. Rémi, S.Thierry, Hautvillers, Verzy and Orbais, were founded in the region. The monks introduced both learning and viticulture, and founded hospices for the sick and for travellers. Wine grew in importance, not only for the sacraments, but also because of the increasing number of visitors drawn to the region: as with beer in England, wine was often drunk because the water was not safe.

During the twelfth century, the knights of Champagne played a prominent role in the First Crusade, and the Second Crusade was largely instigated by S. Bernard at Châlons in 1147. Throughout this period the wines of Champagne grew in popularity, and kings and emperors visited the province to taste them. In 1359, during the Hundred Years War with France, Edward III of England besieged Reims because he wanted to be crowned there. He failed to take the town, but made off with many barrels of wine. In 1417, the Duke of Burgundy laid claim to Champagne, which led to one of the bloodiest and most famous periods of French history. The Burgundians were repulsed by Joan of Arc's army and Charles VII was crowned king in Reims Cathedral. When Henry VII landed in France in 1495, the *vignerons* around Reims were ordered to pull up their vines for fear that the English would use them for cooking, or for filling the moat in order to scale the city walls.

For the next 300 years the province flourished. The kings of France kept agents there to buy the best wines, the nobility built splendid houses there; art and literature flourished. The sixteenth century Steward's Mansion in Châlons is now the Préfecture. Many of the abbeys were rebuilt, only to be destroyed again a century later during the Revolution. A school of sculpture was founded at Troyes and magnificent houses were built in Reims. Henry VIII bought vineyards in Champagne in the sixteenth century, where he had his own presses and envoys to produce wine for the English court.

Champagne became a bloody battleground again towards the end of the eighteenth century, when the country was thrown into war. The Battle of Valmy in 1792 marked the start of Napoléon I's wars, and the struggles ended in Champagne with the Battle of Reims, when the Russians invaded in 1814. They, incidentally, helped to coin the word *bistro*. They would enter inns and thump their hands down on the tables shouting *'Bystro'* (the Russian word for 'quick'). Thus *bistros* were created to serve food and drink quickly.

The Champagne area was not at peace for very long. The Prussians ruled Champagne for a time after Napoléon III's defeat at Sedan in 1870. The Germans invaded again in World War I and Champagne became a battlefield once more; the two battles of the Marne being the most costly. The second battle, in 1918, was decisive, however, in driving the Germans out. The cost was not only counted in lives; the vineyards were destroyed and the ground was scarred with craters and trenches. Replanting was started and in Reims, where four-fifths of the city had been destroyed, rebuilding commenced. Within a few years grapes were being grown again and wine made.

Hostilities in France at the beginning of World War II ended so abruptly that there were no long drawn-out campaigns and Champagne, though invaded, suffered little damage to its vineyards although Reims itself was very badly damaged.

Over the centuries Champagne has continued to produce wine, but originally this wine was a totally different product to the one we know today because it was 'still' rather than 'sparkling'. The growers soon realised that wines with a natural sparkle could be produced, but they had no means of trapping these bubbles in the bottle. An oiled cloth pushed into the neck of the bottle, and then covered with a wax seal, did not form a very efficient stopper. Another method, pouring a small quantity of oil on to the surface of the wine, was even less effective. The growers did not appreciate that after the initial fermentation following the harvest, the wine underwent a second fermentation in the spring, when the temperature again started to rise, and any remaining sugar and yeast started to react together. Consequently, they always bottled their wine after the first fermentation, and then the second would take place, blow out the cloth stoppers, and a large quantity of the produce each year must have been wasted.

It was Pierre Pérignon, a young Benedictine monk from the Abbey at Hautvillers, who solved the problem and established his place in the history of Champagne. He was the cellarmaster at the abbey, and was in charge of making the wine, having been appointed in the late 1660s. He is reputed to have been the first to make a totally still red wine; he was an expert at blending, and produced the first *cuvées* – the blending of wine from different vats. He also re-introduced corks to the district, not used since the Romans left about 1,200 years previously.

Using his scientific training, he also developed a method of controlling the fermentation so that the grapes produced a clear wine, instead of a cloudy one, which still retained its bubbles or *mousse*. Fermentation contributed to another problem, however, because with a cork firmly in place, the bubbles could not escape. As the bubbles increased, the pressure inside the bottle grew so that either the cork was blasted out or the bottle exploded. Previously, although a sparkling wine was being produced, the stoppers were so ineffective that almost all the gases escaped and the end product was, in effect, a still wine. Dom Pérignon developed a tougher glass better able to withstand the build-up of pressure, and used corks able to contain the gases, and so the first true sparkling Champagne was created.

Champagne soon became popular throughout the courts of Europe, and even the occupation of the province by the Russians helped to boost sales. The Russians developed a taste for the sparkling wine and, until their own Revolution, they were Champagne's biggest customers.

The *phylloxera* (insects that feed upon plant juices) which invaded Europe and destroyed the vineyards of France during the last century, attacked Champagne later than other places, so the vineyards were able to go on producing wine long after Bordeaux and Burgundy had ceased production; this, too, boosted their popularity. At this time, most of the Champagne produced was sweet, varying from medium to very sweet. As tastes for drier wines developed, especially in Britain, the first dry Champagnes were produced.

Also at this time, there was concern over the large quantity of Champagne being produced, and moves were made to introduce laws controlling the area of production, the types of grape to be used and so on. Until then, any grape had been allowed, and blenders were able to buy in grapes from a very large area, even outside Champagne, which at that time was much larger than it is today. This attempt to introduce controls led to the 'Champagne riots' of 1910 and 1911, which followed the bad harvest of 1909. Buildings were broken into, and Champagne was tipped into the streets 'where it ran like rivers'. The next two harvests were good, and people once more concentrated on making Champagne.

The Vineyards

The vineyards in Champagne constitute one of the smallest vine-growing areas in France. They cover only one-fiftieth of France's total vineyard area, and run for 144km along the hillsides in belts between 350 metres and 1,400 metres wide. The vines are squat and low-yielding, and only three varieties are allowed: *chardonnay*, a white; and *pinot noir* and *pinot meunier*, both red. About 75 per cent of the vineyards are planted with *pinot*, one of the 'noble' grape varieties, which gives the wine body and backbone. The *chardonnay*, also a 'noble' grape, gives lightness, freshness and elegance.

There are four main vineyard areas: the Montagne de Reims, the Vallée de la Marne, the Côte des Blancs (mostly *chardonnay*), and the Aube in the south. The de-limited area of Champagne covers about 35,000 hectares. At present there are around 28,525ha of grape-bearing vines, with a further 2,020ha not yet in production. Most are owned by the 17,000 or so growers, but about 3,000 hectares are owned by shippers.

All the vineyards producing grapes for Champagne have an official classification – the *Echelle des Crus* – which rates them between 80% and 100%. Villages rated between 90% and 100% are known as *premiers crus* and those at 100% are *grands crus*. These terms frequently appear on labels and are most often used by producers who grow and make their own wines. The higher the *échelle* rating the higher the price the grapes fetch. The *grand cru* villages are: Ambonnay, Avize, Aÿ, Beaumont-sur-Vesle, Bouzy, Chouilly (*chardonnay* only, no red grapes), Cramant, Louvois, Mailly-Champagne, Le Mesnil-sur-Oger, Oger, Oiry, Puisieul, Sillery, Tours-sur-Marne (red grapes only not Chardonnay), Verzenay and Verzy. Chouilly, Le Mesnil-sur-Oger, Oger, Oiry and Verzy were all upgraded from premiers crus in 1985.

The *premier cru* villages and their *échelle* are: Mareuil-sur-Aÿ and Tauxières (99%); Bergères-les-Vertus (only *chardonnay*), Billy-le-Grand, Bisseuil, Chouilly (*pinot* only), Cuis (*chardonnay* only), Dizy, Grauves, Trépail, Vaudemanges, Vertus, Villeneuve-Renneville, Villers-Marmery and Voipreux (all 95%); Chigny-les-Roses, Ludes, Montbré, Rilly-la-Montagne, Taissy and Trois Puits (all 94%); Avenay, Champillon, Cumières, Hautvillers and Montigny (all 93%); Bergères-les-Vertus (*pinot* only), Bezannes, Chamery, Coligny (*chardonnay* only), Cuis (*pinot* only), Eceuil, Etréchy (*chardonnay* only), Grauves (*pinot* only), Jouy-les-Reims, Les Mesneux, Pargny-les-Reims, Pierry, Sacy, Tours-sur-Marne (*chardonnay* only), Villedommange, Villers-Allerand and Villers-aux-Noeuds (all 90%).

After hand-picking, the grapes were traditionally pressed three times. The juice from the first pressing, the *vin de cuvée*, is used to produce the finest Champagnes; the juice from the second, *première taille*, and from the third, *deuxième taille*, were used in blending. The third pressing has now effectively been abolished.

A *cuve* is a vat, and *cuvée* is best described as a blend from various vats. After pressing, the juice is put into vats for about half a day so that the impurities settle on the bottom. Fermentation has already started at this stage because of the action of yeast on sugar, and this is allowed to continue either in wooden vats or stainless steel fermentation tanks. As winter approaches and temperatures fall, the yeasts become less active and fermentation ends. To ensure that this happens, the cellar doors are often opened to let the cold air in. During the winter the wine is racked, usually three times. This means transferring it to another vat in such a way that the sediment is left behind. The winemaster also decides at this time which wines will be used for blending.

Before the spring, the wine is 'fined' by adding whipped egg-white which attracts any remaining sediment. It is filtered and then blended. A *dosage* or *liqueur de tirage*, is added to each bottle to feed the yeast, in order to restart fermentation, and the amount added dictates how bubbly the wine will be. This *dosage* is cane sugar, dissolved in still wine, and 0.14g of sugar produces about one atmosphere of pressure. The bottle is then capped with a metal crown cork able to withstand at least six atmospheres of pressure. This is necessary because of the build-up of gases produced during secondary fermentation.

During the secondary fermentation, sediment also builds up in the bottle, and it was Mme Nicole-Barbe Veuve Clicquot who is credited with developing the system of *remuage* to remove it. The wine bottles are placed in a rack called a *pupitre*. The bottles are placed, neck first, into the rack and every day a *remueur* gives them a slight twist. Very gradually the bottle changes its position until finally its neck points to the ground and contains all the sediment. This is a very skilled job, and a *remueur* can turn up to 30,000 bottles in a day. The process takes a long time, however – sometimes as long as twelve weeks. Computer-controlled machines now do much of this work, and once loaded, can do the same job round the clock, seven days a week. The machine has speeded up the process to between one week and ten days.

Once the sediment has all been shaken to the neck of the bottle, it has to be disposed of. This is done by dipping the neck in a freezing solution which solidifies the sediment. The cap is then removed and the frozen sediment shoots out because of the pressure behind it. Some wine is inevitably lost in the process, but the bottle level is topped up and a second dosage added, sometimes with a drop of added brandy. The sweetness of this dosage dictates the sweetness of the finished product. The bottle is then corked and wired, and is ready for dispatch or further maturation in the cellars.

There are so many different styles of champagne produced that I find it a little foolish when someone says he once tried champagne and did not like it, so has never tried it again. There is, among the hundreds of champagnes produced, something for virtually everyone.

Most champagne sold is non-vintage, which must be bottled for at least one year. The same House can produce several different styles. You will also see Buyers' Own Brands (BOB), which are blended to suit customers' demands, and may be produced for a hotel chain, supermarket or other client. If you are rich enough you can even have your own champagne specially created for you.

Vintage champagnes, at least three years old and often very much older, are only produced after the best harvests and are always dry, or *brut*. While vintage champagne should be the product of a single year, some Houses do add a small amount from previous years to try to produce a consistent style. A good vintage will last for many years, but exactly how long will depend on the maker. About ten years is a good rule, because it is best to drink wines on the way up to their peak, rather than on the way down. Some vintage wines, however, have great longevity.

Pink or *rosé* champagne became very fashionable

after World War II. It can be made from *pinot noir* grapes, by allowing the juice to remain in contact with the grape skins long enough for it to take some of their colouring, but the more usual way is to mix a local red wine with the champagne just before bottling. The wine of Bouzy is widely used, but others include Ambonnay, Aÿ, Cumières, Dizy, Rilly, Verzenay and Villedommange.

Most champagne is made from a blend of red and white grapes. If it is a result of using only white grapes, it is called *blanc de blancs*, and if only red grapes are used, it is known as *blanc de noire*. Many of the champagne Houses now offer *cuvée de prestige*, produced only for special occasions. The wines are the finest which can be produced, and no expense is spared. *Crémant* is the final category and this has only half the pressure of normal champagne and is therefore less gassy. It has become very fashionable in the past few years.

The other wines of Champagne

In addition to sparkling wines, Champagne produces still wines; red, white and *rosé* under the *Coteaux Champenois Appellation Contrôlée*. The wine must be made only from the three grape varieties allowed in Champagne, and must follow all other conditions laid down by the Champagne AC.

In Champagne the maximum yield is 13,000kg per hectare, and the quantity which may be used for the production of sparkling champagne is fixed every year. The remainder can then be used for the *Coteaux Champenois*. If growers want to boost stocks of champagne after a poor harvest, they will use most of the production for sparkling wines, so the quantity of *Coteaux Champenois* varies greatly from year to year. They tend to be very acidic wines, but can be very fine. They are worth drinking when visiting the area since most of the produce is consumed there – only just over a quarter of the production being exported.

Another wine well worth trying is the *Rosé des*

Riceys. It comes from the southernmost part of the Champagne region, in the Aube, and is made only from the *pinot noir* grape. Only in certain years, when the grapes reach the correct ripeness, is it made. The grapes are not pressed initially, but put into a vat where their own weight squeezes the juice out. This juice, which is already fermenting, is then pumped over all the grapes until the winemaker is satisfied that the colour is right. The juice is then run off and fermentation allowed to continue in the normal way. The resulting wine has the most incredible colour, often described as 'a red sky at sunset'. It is austere, with a flavour of gooseberries. It is one of the rarest wines you can come across, and is therefore very expensive.

Ratafia is made in Champagne, and is usually drunk as an apéritif. It is made by adding wine alcohol, usually to cognac, to freshly-pressed wine juice. It produces a sweet drink of 18-22° of alcohol. There is also *Marc de Champagne*, a fiery spirit of 40° of alcohol and more, made from the *marc*, which is the pulp of the grape skins, seeds and stalks left after the last pressing. The *marc* is pressed, and the juice extracted is then distilled.

The Law

The Champagne laws are so strict that even the amount of juice to be extracted at each pressing is laid down. From 4,000 kg of grapes, no more than 2,666 litres of juice or 'must' can be extracted if it is to bear the name of 'Champagne'. From the first pressing 2,050 litres of juice may be extracted, and 500 litres of 'vin de taille', instead of the previous total of 2,666 litres – enough for one cask. Many of the best producers belong to the *Syndicat de Grandes Marques de Champagne*, and their wines are known as *grandes marques*, but like many of the official listings, the *Syndicat* has one or two members who have allowed things to slip a little, while there are many eminently suitable candidates for membership waiting in the wings.

The *Comité Interprofessionnel du Vin de Champagne* (CIVC) is the authority responsible for co-ordinating the interests of the many thousands of individual vineyard owners and their workers with those of the commercial outlets for the finished product – Champagne. Established by the French Ministry of Agriculture and Viticulture in 1941, its basic task over the years has been to ensure the maintenance of the outstanding quality of the wine, even at the expense of the quantity produced. This means strict controls over the areas within the province of Champagne where vines bearing only approved grapes may be grown. The de-limited area is distinctive for the quality of the soil, its climate and the basic underlay of a particular kind of chalk, none of which is found in this combination in any other part of the world. Its main function, however, is to protect the *Appellation*, and it is quick to take action against anything which may interfere with Champagne's reputation as 'the Wine of Kings and the King of Wines'.

The CIVC also advises growers on new viticultural and wine-making developments, and how to tackle outbreaks of plant disease. Its technical team constantly monitor and report on what is happening in the different vine-growing regions which make up Champagne. The CIVC has a large research staff and its own experimental vineyards, winery and cellars, as well as extensive quality-control laboratories.

For the last 30 years, under the terms and conditions of an inter-professional contract between the growers and the Champagne producers, the CIVC have convened meetings before each annual harvest to agree a figure for the grapes. For the three years 1990-93 the Champagne industry is operating a new 'more flexible structure', with a free market price for grapes. The CIVC is responsible for setting a reference price before each harvest, and monitors prices during the picking, on a daily basis. The principle elements of the new system are:

a free price for grapes, based on a price reference

established annually by the CIVC;

each buyer is given a 'ceiling', based on the volume of the harvest and level of champagne sales.

Day to day transactions are registered by the CIVC;

The growers who have pledged grapes to the Houses have a guarantee of purchase and price.

In 1990 the reference price was fixed at 32 French francs, although the free market determined the price at 36 francs, a 34 per cent increase over 1989. The higher price of grapes, albeit for wine which will not be sold until 1993, had an immediate impact on retail prices. In the first six months of 1991, champagne shippers raised their prices in the UK by 12 – 14 per cent. The retail price increase was correspondingly higher and, in some cases, very much greater. Of some concern is the fact that while there have also been price increases in the United States, they have certainly not been of the same magnitude, which suggests that some retailers have been cashing in. As a result, sales of champagne in the UK for the first six months of 1991 were down by 51 per cent.

It is generally agreed that higher prices will reduce demand and that will relieve pressure on the suppliers. Exports are unlikely to match the 1990 levels again, certainly not for the foreseeable future, and the champagne Houses can concentrate all their attention on maintaining quality without the diversion of wondering how they can cope with demand.

The turmoil of the last two years has caused a fundamental re-think in champagne – the lessons of the 1980s have been learnt. Corners cannot be cut and consumers are not prepared to go on paying ever-rising prices for a product which, in some instances, has suffered a reduction in quality.

A new sense of reality has emerged in Champagne, and growers, producers and consumers should all benefit in the years ahead as quality again becomes paramount.

The Vineyard Year

November.	Unwanted vine shoots are cut back and fertiliser is applied.
December-February.	A quiet time. Manure is applied, new topsoil added.
March-April.	Pruning takes place. Posts and wires are repaired.
May.	First spraying takes place.
June.	Flowering takes place. Further spraying, hoeing between vines and removal of excess foliage.
July.	Hoeing continues, further spraying if necessary, and more foliage is removed to increase airflow and reduce risk of mould or rot.
August-September.	The ripening months, more leaves are removed to expose the grapes to the sun.
October.	Harvesting time, usually 100 days after flowering and about the middle of the month.

The Winery

First fermentation: this takes place in stainless steel tanks or oak barrels at a constant temperature. When the fermentation has finished (about 3 weeks later) the wine is racked. It is then exposed to a colder temperature which helps the sediment settle, leaving the wine clear. The wine is then drawn off from the sediment.

The *cuvée* (blending): wines from as many as thirty or forty different vineyards are 'married' together to create a particular House style. In the case of a non-vintage, wines from several years are included in the blend, whereas for a vintage, only wine from one year can be used.

Second fermentation: after natural fermenting

agents have been introduced into the blend, the wine is bottled and stacked in the cellars – where the transformation from a still to a sparkling wine takes place.

The *remuage*: helped by the coolness of the cellars, a sediment collects in the bottle during the slow ageing process. After the statutory time in the cellars the bottles are placed neck downwards in racks. Skilled operators twist, shake and turn each bottle daily. This has the effect of moving the sediment slowly but surely into the neck of the bottle. The whole operation takes between six weeks and three months. The bottles are then stacked neck down waiting for the *dégorgement*.

The *dégorgement*: To remove the sediment from the bottle the neck is placed in a vat containing freezing brine which creates a block of ice in the neck. The sediment is trapped in the ice which is ejected when the cap is removed. The bottle is then toppe d up with a little cane sugar, some older wine known as the *dosage*, and a cork is fitted.

Understanding the Label
The following items of information must appear on the label:

1. The word Champagne

2. Brand name

3. Sugar content
The amount of residual sugar in the wine determines its category:

Demi-Sec:	33-50g
Sec:	17-35g
Extra Dry:	12-20g
Brut:	under 15g
Extra-Brut	0-6g

4. Nominal Value (the amount of wine in the container). Champagne can be sold in quarter-litre bottles (20 cl), half-bottles (37.5 cl) and bottles (75cl). Larger sizes are:

Magnum	equivalent to	2 bottles
Jeroboam		4 bottles
Rheoboam		6 bottles
Methuselah		8 bottles
Salmanazar		12 bottles
Balthazar		16 bottles
Nebuchadnezzar		20 bottles

5. Alcohol Content, as a percentage of volume. This can vary between a minimum of 10% volume (11% volume for vintage wines) and a maximum of 13%.

6. Professional Registration Code:
   The following professional registration code was agreed in 1990 by the Comité Interprofessionnel du Vin de Champagne (CIVC) and each producer's code must appear on the label.
   If the producer owns the brand name, the initials used are:

NM	indicates a	Négociant-Manipulant, a Champagne House
CM	" "	Coopérative de Manipulation, a Champagne from a Cooperative
RM	" "	Récoltant-Manipulant, a grower producing Champagne from his own grapes
RC	" "	Récoltant-Coopérateur, a new designation for a grower selling Champagne produced by a cooperative
SR	" "	Société de Récoltant, a new designation for a company created by wine growers who are members of the same family

In all other cases, labels carry the code: MA indicating Marque d'Acheteur: or Buyers' Own Brand (BOB).

7. Producer

8. Location of producer

9. Country of origin.

Champagne etiquette

Storing

Although the experts disagree, I think that all champagne, both vintage and non-vintage, benefits from ageing provided it is stored correctly.

Non-vintage champagne can soften remarkably if stored for half a year or so. Many vintages benefit from two or three years' keeping after release. Exceptional vintages benefit from much longer storage.

In all cases the wines must be stored in the dark at a steady cool temperature. The three things to avoid are light, movement and fluctuating temperatures.

Opening

The secret in opening a bottle of champagne is to turn the bottle and not the cork. The more vigorous you are, the more it will spray everywhere.

1. Hold the bottle at a forty-five-degree angle away from you and carefully remove the foil and wire mesh over the cork, while placing your thumb firmly over the cork.
2. With the bottle still pointing at an angle, grip the cork tightly in one hand and gently rotate the bottle with the other, holding it firmly near the base.
3. The twisting action should move the cork a little and it can then be carefully and slowly removed. Keep the bottle at forty-five-degrees while doing this and do not let the cork pop out by itself as it will be closely followed by a fountain of escaping champagne. Some people insert the end of a spoon or fork into the newly opened bottle to prevent it frothing over.

Serving

Champagne should only be served in the tall 'flute' glass, not the wide, broad-rimmed *coupe*, which is so often seen on television and in films. The *coupe* is said to have been modelled on the breast of Marie Antoinette at a time when champagne was a still wine.

The large surface area of the glass allows the bubbles to escape quickly and the wine soon becomes flat.

The flute comes in a number of styles but all are designed to compliment the champagne. The mouth of the glass should be narrower than its centre, to concentrate the bouquet and prevent the bubbles from escaping too quickly.

Ideally champagne should be served at around 8 °C, and it is better to cool it down slowly in an ice bucket containing both water and ice. You can keep bottles in the fridge if you are a frequent imbiber. If champagne is served too cold it will lose much of its bouquet. Pour champagne slowly, topping up each glass in stages to allow the froth to settle.

I am often asked what is the best champagne to drink for a particular occasion, and there is no hard-and-fast answer. You must drink what you like and what you can afford. If you are hosting a party you may not want to drink the most expensive champagnes all night, but you could choose a better wine for toasts. The following pages will show you just how many champagnes and different styles there are to choose from. I hope there will be many discoveries to be made – and enjoyed.

The Champagne Houses

HENRI ABELÉ

50 Rue de Sillery, BP 18 - 51051 Reims
Tel: 26 85 23 86

History. One of the oldest of the Champagne Houses, founded in 1757 by Théodore Vander Veken. His son Rémi took over in 1799 expanded, his ownership of vineyards in Rilly-la-Montagne and built up sizeable exports to the Low Countries and Italy. In 1834 Rémi's nephew Auguste Ruinart de Brimont, who had taken over six years earlier, joined forces with Antoine de Müller, former cellarmaster at Veuve Cliquot where, with the Widow, he helped create the system of *remouage*. The Champagne became very popular with the German aristocracy and earned the name Gotterwein 'The wine of the Gods'. The firm then passed to Francois Abelé de Müller and in 1842 moved to Ludes. Henri took over in 1876 on his father's death and moved back to Reims. In 1903 the company merged with its original founders to become Abelé-Van der Veken; in 1942 it was taken over by the Compagnie Française des Grands Vin and in 1985 was bought by Freixenet, the massive Spanish wine group, and one of the world's largest makers of sparkling wines. The champagne is still marketed under the Henri Abelé *marque*. Production has been cut back as more attention is focused on quality. Cellars have been extended and the winery upgraded.

Visiting:	None.
Vineyards:	None
Annual Prod:	750,000 bottles
Exports:	35-40%

House Style:	Becoming softer but still pronounced *chardonnay* character – elegant, fresh and flowery

NV Brut Sourire de Reims (40-60% PM, 30-40% PN, 10-30% Ch)
Average bottle age 2-2^1/$_2$ yrs. light gold colour, fresh, attractive, flowery, fine bubbles, elegant *NV Grande Marque* .

NV Rosé Brut (33% PN, 33% PM, 33% Ch)
Own cultured yeasts are used and malolactic fermentation is induced. Red wine is added. Full bodied but still fresh and fruity; good *pinot noir* characteristics.

Demi-Sec (40-60% PM, 30-40% PN, 10-30% Ch)
Average bottle age 2-2^1/$_2$yrs, cane sugar added.
Light gold colour, fresh, floral, fine bubbles, elegant.

Blanc de Blancs (100% Ch). Only produced in outstanding vintages. Floral, light gold colour, elegant, touch of aggressiveness.

Grand Marque Impériale Brut (20-30% PM, 50-60% PN, 30-40% Ch)
Age before shipping 4-6yrs, current vintage 1982 (recommended previous vintages 1980, 1976, 1975, 1969). Fresh, balanced, well structured, but not that special.

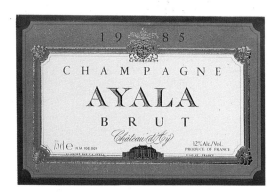

CHAMPAGNE AYALA

Chateau D'Aÿ, 2 Boulevard du Nord, 51160 Aÿ Tel: 26 55 15 44

History. One of great old names of champagne, the House was founded in 1860 by Edmond de Ayala, the son of a Columbian diplomat posted to Paris. He married Berthe, niece of the Vicomte de Mareuil. Her dowry included several fine vineyards, and Champagne Ayala was established to sell the wines produced.

In 1937 the firm was taken over by René Chayoux, already owner of the champagne Houses Duminy and Montebello. Since his death in 1969, it has been run by Jean-Michel Ducellier.

Visiting:	The cellars can be visited by appointment.
Vineyards:	25 hectares which are part of Montebello Estate at Mareuil-sur-Aò, planted with *pinot noir*, and St.Martin d'Ablois, planted with *pinot meunier*. These provide about 20% of their needs.
Annual Prod:	1 million bottles.
Exports:	45-50% and increasing as the Far East market expands.

House Style: *Pinot noir* accounts for the largest
percentage of the blend and the wines
are characterised by their fruitiness,
balance and finesse. Very good value. A
Grande Marque.

NV Demi-Sec (50-60% PN, 15-25% Ch, 25% PM).
very clean, fruity bouquet. Fruity, perfumed and sweet on the
palate, well balanced.

NV Brut (50% PN, 20-25% PM, 20-25% Ch)
Pleasing yeasty fruitiness, firm, clean palate with *pinot noir*
influence, good acidity.

NV Brut Rosé (100% PN)
Soft and fruity with hint of raspberries in the bouquet.
Rounded and delicious but finishes short.

Brut 1985 (70-75% PN, 25-30% Ch).
Elegant, fruity, floral bouquet, much more depth of fruit than
the NV. Good acidity and excellent balance, strong finish.
Improves with age. Previous vintages 1983, 1982, 1979,
1975, 1973.

Blanc de Blanc Brut 1985 (100% Ch)
Very delicate greeny gold colour, fragrant, floral nose,
creamy mousse, high acidity. Recommended previous
vintages 1982, 1979, 1975.

Grande Cuvée Ayala 1985 (75-80% Ch, 20-25% PN)
Surprisingly youthful, fruity bouquet with hints of apple and
nutty, biscuity *chardonnay* taste. Only made in the best years.
Classy and elegant and continues to improve after bottling.

BARANCOURT

**Brice, Martin et Tritant, Place André Tritant,
Bouzy, 51150 Tours-sur-Marne
Tel: 26 59 00 67**

History. Three growers, Jean-Paul Brice, Pierre Martin
and Raynald Tritant joined forces in 1966 to sell their
champagne, made from the wines of Bouzy. Three years
later they realised they needed a good brand name, and
chose Barancourt, a once-famous House which had ceased
trading on the death of Philogone Barancourt in 1941. The
Barancourt name is one of the oldest names in Bouzy and
the three young men acquired the *marque* by purchasing
some of the vineyards owned by the House. As soon as the
partnership was forged, the three growers started to replant
vineyards abandoned during the *phylloxera* outbreak, and
when the House of Barancourt was launched in 1969, all
their respective holdings were merged as Domaine de
Barancourt.

In 1975 they decided to restructure their business and
founded the company Brice, Martin et Tritant, although
still using the brandname Barancourt. At the end of the
1960s and the beginning of the 1970s, when very few
people were really investing in Champagne, they acquired
large acreages in the Aube and, whenever possible, bought
any small parcels of vineyards in Bouzy and Cramant
which came on the market. As a result they now own
about 82 ha of vineyards producing all three champagne
varieties but they do not use any of their *pinot meunier* in
their own wines.

There has been a major investment programme, especially in pressing equipment in Bouzy, Cramant, Merrey, Baroville and Colombé-le Sec. The House holds stocks of around 3.1 million litres and annual production of Barancourt is about 550,000 bottles. The rest of their produce is sold to other *négociants*.

Visiting:	Cellars and wine shop open daily. Groups of up to 60 can be accommodated by appointment.
Vineyards:	About 82 ha: 15 ha Bouzy (13ha PN, 2ha Ch); 12.5 ha Cramant (all Ch); 20 ha Baroville (all PN); 12.5 ha Merrey-sur-Arce (5 ha PN, 3 ha Ch, 4.5 ha PM); 22 ha Landreville (13 ha Ch, 6 ha PN, 4.5 ha PM); and 15 ha rented in Loches-sur-Ource (all PN).
Annual Prod:	350,000 bottles
Exports:	30%.
House Style:	Refined and well balanced. Firm, fruity, youthful wines which need time to mature fully.

NV Brut Réserve (80% PN, 20% Ch)
A firm vigorous *mousse* and attractive *pinot* nose. A youthful wine with good acidity and abundance of ripe *pinot* fruit to balance. A good finisher.

NV Demi-Sec Réserve (80% PN, 20% Ch)
A well-balanced wine, not overly sweet with good fruit and acidity, and a long, fruity honeyed finish.

NV Blanc de Blancs Brut (100% Ch)
A very elegant wine, with fine delicate mousse and soft,
creamy, aromatic nose. Lots of rich, ripe fruit on the palate
but very light and balanced. Will develop more
complexity with a little more bottle age.

NV Rosé Brut (85% Ch, 15% PN)
A big rosé in every sense. Dark-coloured with creamy,
fruity nose and full-bodied, mouth-filling red fruit
flavours; but still very elegant. A long, strong finish.

Vintage 1985 Brut (100% Ch)
Very elegant, with fine, persistent *mousse*. Attractive soft,
fruity nose with vanilla and toasty aromas. Rich, and fruity
on the palate. Good balance and complexity. A long
lingering finish.

Cramant Brut Grand Cru NV (100% Ch from Cramant)
Light and elegant, with fine, persistent *mousse* and
creamy, fruity, aromatic nose with hints of vanilla and
brioche. Light, soft fruit on the palate, well-balanced with
a stylish finish.

Bouzy Brut Grand Cru NV (80% PN, 20% Ch, both from
Bouzy)
Another big wine but remarkably elegant. A firm vigorous
mousse with *pinot* fruit dominating the nose and palate,
and a very long, full finish.

Cuvée des Fondateurs 1985 (85% Ch from Cramant, 15%
PN from Bouzy)
A wine of great finesse and elegance. A fine but persistent
mousse and very attractive nose with complex floral and
fruit aromas. Great balance and complexity on the palate
with soft fruit, good acidity and a long finish.

CHAMPAGNE BEAUMET

3 Rue Malakoff, BP 247, 51207 Epernay
Tel: 26 59 50 10

History. The House of Beaumet was established in 1878 by the Beaumet family in the village of Pierry, and later moved to larger premises in Châlons-sur-Marne. In 1977 M. Jacques Trouillard took over the company and the House of Beaumet now operates from offices and cellars in the beautiful Malakoff Park in the centre of Epernay. The House controls eighty hectares of vineyards in the best locations of the Champagne district, especially in the Côtes des Blancs. The cellars and buildings were constructed at the end of last century and rebuilt in 1981 when all equipment and machinery was modernised. The firm has close links with Jeanmaire and Oudinot.

Visiting:	By appointment.
Vineyards:	80 ha: Avize (10 ha) Cramant (8 ha) and Chouilly (12 ha), all 100% *chardonnay*; Tauxiéres (8 ha), Les Mesneux (3ha), Villedommange (3 ha), Orbais-l'Abbaye (7.5 ha), Reims (4.5 ha), Dizy (5 ha), Champillon (7 ha), and others (12 ha), almost all *pinot noir*.
Annual Prod:	1.5 million bottles.
Exports:	Most of the production is for export, especially to Britain and the US.

House Style: Fresh, fruity, floral wines, with
                  complexity and ageing.

NV Brut (40% PN, 30% PM, 30% Ch)
A blend of thirty wines aged for at least three years to
allow aromas to develop. Golden-yellow colour , fine and
persistent *mousse*, fruity nose, fresh, elegant and good
balance.

Blanc de Noirs 1985 (85% PN, 15% PM)
A blend of wines from ten different vineyards in the
Montagne de Reims, all 100% *grand cru*. Aged for at
least four years. Brilliant golden-yellow, small and
persistent *mousse*, big, aromatic bouquet with lots of
fruit, full-bodied, fruity but elegant.

Rosé Brut (70% PN, 30% PM)
Aged for at least three years to develop full aromas. Dark
pink, small but persistent *mousse*, aromatic, fruity
bouquet, crisp, fresh and lingering.

Rosé 1985 (100% PN)
Aged for minimum four years. Brilliant onion-skin
colour, small but persistent *mousse*, elegant taste with
hints of red fruit.

Brut 1985 (55% PN, 35% Ch, 10% PM)
A blend of twenty different *cuvées* from the Montagne de
Reims and Côte de Blancs, all 100% *grand cru*. Yellow-
gold colour, with fine and persistent *mousse*. Elegant,
floral, fruity complex nose. Fresh and fruity on the palate
with complexity and long finish.

Blanc de Blancs 1982 Cuvée Malakoff (100% Ch)
Aged for a minimum of seven years. A blend of *grands
crus* from the Côtes des Blancs. Deep yellow colour with
tints of green and a very fine, abundant, persistent
mousse. Elegant complex nose with traces of toast, nuts
and lime. Lots of fruit but great finesse and a long finish.

BESSERAT DE BELLEFON

**Allée du Vignoble, RN 51, Murigny, Reims
Tel: 26 06 09 18**

History. Founded in 1843 in Aÿ by Edmond Besserat, the
House did not really grow until the 1920s when his two
sons, Edmond (who married Yvonne de Bellefon, hence
the expanded House name) and Victor, launched their
Crémant Brut. The firm was the first to specialise in
commercial quantities of *crémant*. In 1959 the House was
sold to Cinzano and a period of dramatic growth
followed. The firm acquired the House of Salon, a *grande
marque*, and in 1970 moved to new cellars at Murigny on
the outskirts of Reims. In 1976 the House was sold to the
giant Pernod-Ricard and the emphasis in the past few
years has been to boost exports. *Crémants* account for
about forty per cent of sales.

Visiting:	Visitors are welcome but should phone to check opening times.
Vineyards:	11 ha (10 ha of PN in Aÿ, 1 ha of Ch at Le Mesnil-sur-Oger).
Annual Prod:	2.2 million bottles.
Exports:	400,000 bottles.
House Style:	Flowery, lively, light and well-balanced. Very fine *crémants*.

Brut NV (50% PN, 20% PM, 30% Ch)
Strong, vigorous *mousse*, dominant *pinot* nose, big and
fruity with good acidity.

Vintage Brut 1982 (50% PN, 50% Ch)
Big, long and complex, mouth-filling fresh intense fruit,
yet well-balanced, mature and elegant.

Crémant Blanc Brut NV (60% Ch)
Very elegant, light and creamy, full of fruit and pleasing
acidity. Best drunk young.

*Cuvée des Moines Rosé Brut NV (50% PN, 10-15% PM,
35-40% Ch)*
Great finesse, fruity, youthful and great balance. Drinks
excellently young or with a little age.

Cuvée Prestige Blanc de Blancs (80% PN, 20% Ch)
Light and lively, creamy and flowery with full fruit. Very

good balance of freshness and fruit.

Brut Intégral 1979 (50% PN, 50% Ch)
A non-*dosage* wine that must be served at the correct
temperature (11-12°C). Almost smoky nose with a fine,
vigorous *mousse*. Surprising depth and finesse, and
excellent with delicately flavoured foods.

BILLECART-SALMON

40 Rue Carnot, 51160 Mareuil-sur-Aÿ
Tel: 26 52 60 22

History. Founded in 1818 the Billecart family has lived in
Mareuil-sur-Aÿ since the mid-sixteenth century. The
House was established when Nicolas-François Billecart
married Elisabeth Salmon. The *grande marque* quickly
established an international reputation with a US
subsidiary set up in the early 1840s. The US agency,
however, handled the business badly and cost the House a
small fortune, which set the company back for many
years. Russia became the company's major export market
but this trade, too, collapsed after the 1917 revolution.
Eight years later the decision was made to sell off the
firm's vineyards and the money raised was invested in the
winery and cellars. The fifth generation of the family still
own and run the company.

Visiting:	By appointment only.
Vineyards:	None. All grapes are purchased from Champagne's 25 top vineyards with 40% from the Côte des Blancs, 30% from Montagne de Reims, and 30% from the Vallée de la Marne.
Annual Prod:	500,000 bottles
Exports:	50%.
House Style:	Light, fragrant and full-flavoured. Great complexity and longevity.

Brut NV (41% PM, 34% PN, 25% Ch)
Elegant and well-balanced, crisp but not completely dry.
Floral, lemony and mouth-filling, with long, strong finish.
There is also a *NV Sec* and *NV Demi-Sec*.

Brut Rosé NV (60% PN, 40% Ch)
First produced in 1830, this champagne has been a
mainstay of the Billecart House ever since and now
accounts for fifteen per cent of all production. Very
popular in the US, not least because of its amazing light
salmon-pink colour. Delicate scent, elegant, biscuity
flavours and great finesse.

Brut Vintage Cuvée N.F. Billecart 1985 (60% PN, 40% Ch)
Named in honour of its founder (the great-great-grandfather of the present Director, Jean Roland). Light golden colour, small, persistent *mousse* and *pinot* -dominated nose. A big, rich but elegant wine, mouth-filling and long finish.

Brut Blanc de Blancs Vintage 1985 (100% Ch)
Fine but vigorous *mousse*, flowery nose with hints of hawthorn, ripe *chardonnay* fruit matched by a light, delicate freshness. Delicious with a long, delicate finish.

GAETAN BILLIARD

14-16 Rue de Moissons, 51100 Reims
Tel: 26 47 01 54

History. Founded in 1935 by Gaetan Billiard, a former cellarman, who died in 1967.

Visiting:	By appointment.
Vineyards:	2 ha which account for about 10-15% of production.
Annual Prod:	85,000 bottles.
Exports:	15-20%.
House Style:	Well-made, well-blended, up-front wines, but not outstanding.

NV Brut (80% PN with some PM, 20% Ch)
Dry and slightly austere, but well balanced. Also *NV Sec* and *Demi-Sec*.

NV Brut Rosé (exact Ch/PN/PM blend not disclosed)
A blended wine with a little red wine added to produce the salmon-pink colour. Softness is compensated for by the lively *mousse*.

Vintage Brut (75-80% PN/PM, 20-25% Ch) and *Vintage Blanc de Blancs Brut* (100% Ch)
These are produced in small quantities and are now gaining wider distribution in export markets.

BOIZEL

14 Rue de Bernon, 51200 Epernay
Tel: 26 55 21 51

History. Evelyne Roques-Boizel took over control of the firm in 1985 and is the only woman controlling a champagne House. She is the fifth generation of Boizels to head the family firm.

The House was founded in 1834 by Auguste Boizel and his wife Julie in Epernay. England soon became their major export market. In 1860 their son Edouard had the huge cellars dug in the chalk of Bernon Mount, and he built the offices and family home above them. By 1945 only the cellars remained and work started on rebuilding the company and its stocks. In 1984 Evelyne succeeded her mother as President and has been responsible for the rapid growth since then.

Oenologist Pascal Vautier has been responsible for introducing the most modern wine-making techniques and creating the new Boizel style. The House also produces a number of 'buyer's own' champagnes. The cellars contain a magnificent collection of very old vintages.

Visiting:	Only customers, by appointment.
Vineyards:	None. Grapes are bought from about fifty villages, allowing a wide choice for the *cuvée* which gives the wines their complexity.

Annual Prod:	1.65 million bottles.
Exports:	50%, with UK the leading importer.

House Style:	Rich, elegant, complex wines with great balance owing to skilful blending.

Brut Rosé (50% PN, 40% PM, 10% Ch)
A reddish-pink colour with lots of fruity *pinot* in the nose, and a mouth-filling crispness. Good balance and long finish.

Brut Réserve (55% PN, 15% PM, 30% Ch)
Soft, fruity bouquet. A touch of toastiness, lots of mouth-filling ripe fruit and good balance.

Brut Blanc de Blancs (100% Ch from the Côte des Blancs)
This *cuvée* was re-launched to celebrate the centenary of the House of Boizel. Rich golden colour with pale green tints. Delicate and elegant but with lots of fruit.

Grand Vintage 1985 (70% PN, 30% Ch)
Classy *pinot* nose. Elegant, soft, fruity *chardonnay* on the palate with *pinot* body for good balance. Needs time.

Joyau de France (65% PN, 35% Ch)
Their prestige *cuvée*. Rich, complex bouquet. A big elegant wine with long finish and long life.

J. BOLLINGER

16 Rue Jules Lobet, 51160 Aÿ
Tel: 26 50 12 34

History. Bollinger is one of the great names in champagne and the House was founded in 1829, in Aÿ, by 26-year-old Jacques Bollinger who was born in Württemburg. He had already been working in the champagne trade for seven years, selling in Germany the wines of the House of Müller-Ruinart, which was founded by his fellow German Antoine Müller in 1822. Müller had worked at Veuve Clicquot and is credited, together with the Widow, of developing *remouage*.

Because of his sales experience, Jacques was approached by the Comte de Villermont and asked to set up a champagne House to sell the wines from his vineyards. These had already developed a reputation abroad, especially in the Channel Islands. Jacques Bollinger established the House with Paul Renaudin, and because the Comte thought it demeaning to have his name associated with a trade, the wines were sold, even until quite recently, under the label of Renaudin, Bollinger and Co.

In 1837 Jacque married the Comte's daughter Louise-Charlotte and set about building up the business. The vineyard acreage was extended with a new planting at Verzenay. On Jacque's death in 1888, his two sons Georges and Joseph continued the expansion with further vineyards established at Bouzy, Louvois and Tauxières.

The House has remained under family control ever

since and is now headed by Christian Bizot and Ghislain de Montgolfier. Both are nephews of the late but legendary Mme Lily Bollinger who was in charge from 1941-1977, and was responsible for the major expansion programme which included the doubling of production. Mme Bollinger travelled the world promoting both champagne and the House of Bollinger, though when she was not jet-setting she could normally be seen cycling around the district.

Visiting:	By appointment only.
Vineyards:	143.5 ha.- 93.73 ha in the Montagne de Reims (Aÿ, Bouzy, Verzenay), 24.85 ha in the Côtes des Blancs (Cuis and Grauves), and 16.1 ha in the Vallée de la Marne (Champvoisy). There are also 8.85 ha of unplanted vineyards. Throughout its history Bollinger has developed a vineyard estate which is the backbone both of the quality of its wines and its reputation. Depending on the vintage, the vineyards supply 60-70% of their needs which guarantees consistency and continuity in both supplies and quality. All the reserve wines are held in magnum and stocks held are the equivalent of five years sales.
Annual Prod:	1.5 million bottles.
Exports:	80%.
House Style:	The wines are vinified in oak to give them their special characteristics and a good proportion of reserve wines are added to ensure consistency and quality. Big characterful wines with plenty of body, depth and length.

Bollinger Special Cuvée Brut (65% PN, 30% Ch, 5% PM)
Well-balanced, combining roundness and freshness, body and elegance. Absolutely biscuity, in style thanks to up to 9% of reserve wine. The wine ages on its lees in the bottle for up to four years before *dégorgement*.

Bollinger Grande Année 1985 (65% PN, 35% Ch)
Only made in exceptional years, when the wine matures on its sediment in the bottle for up to seven years. Typical biscuity, nutty Bollinger nose. Dry, well-balanced, mouth-

CHAMPAGNE

BOLLINGER

SPECIAL CUVÉE

BRUT

12% Vol.   PRODUCE OF FRANCE   75cl

ELABORÉ PAR BOLLINGER · AY · FRANCE

filling with abundant fruit and a long, rounded finish.

Bollinger Grande Année Rosé 1983 (65% PN, 35% Ch plus a little red wine)
A marvellous *rosé* from the House which always swore that the only good champagne was white. Very classy, lovely, nutty, woody nose and big, full, fruity taste. Good acidity, full of flavour and very long finish.

Bollinger RD 1982 (70% PN, 30% Ch)
Aged for an average ten years on its lees and disgorged shortly before release, thus RD for *récemment dégorgé.* The date of disgorgement is declared on the back label. Well-structured and full but with surprising freshness and rich vanilla aromas. Extra ageing adds complexity and extra length on the palate. Rich and elegant with good ageing potential, but at its peak when still bursting with freshness.

Bollinger RD Année Rare (70% PN, 30% Ch, perhaps a little PM)
As above but kept for even longer on its lees for greater body, depth and richness. Even so, still wonderfully fresh.

Bollinger Vieilles Vignes Françaises 1985 (100% PN)
The grapes come from a single vineyard planted with ungrafted *pinot noir* vines. Huge mouth-filling wine with a lot of weight, depth and long finish. Elegant and flowery with great longevity.

BONNAIRE

105 Rue du Carrouge, Cramant, 51200 Epernay
Tel: 26 57 50 85

History. André Bonnaire has an ultra-modern winery producing wines from his 13 ha of vines around Cramant.

Visiting:	Weekdays 8 am-12 noon, and 2-6 p.m.
Vineyards:	13 ha in and around Cramant.
Annual Prod:	100,000 bottles
Exports:	15%.

House Style:	Wines of youthful vigour, freshness and crispness. Much use is made of the Cramant *chardonnay* grapes for delicacy and elegance.

NV Brut (mostly PM with Ch)
A young, lively, easy-drinking wine with rich, fruity nose and full, fruity flavours on the palate. Crisp and full-bodied with a good finish.

NV Blanc de Blancs (100% Ch)
Elegant with lovely soft, ripe-fruit nose and touches of vanilla. Good depth of fruit on the palate and a long, lingering, clean finish.

NV Rosé Brut (predominantly Ch with red wine for colouring)
A lively wine with attractive delicate, floral, almost perfumed nose and good rich fruit on the palate. Vigorous with good depth and a long, crisp finish.

Spécial Club Blanc de Blancs Brut 1983 (100% Ch)
Made only from Cramant wines and still very youthful but with good balance and depth. Appealing soft-fruit nose and full of flavour on the palate with a good finish.

F. BONNET

Route du Mesnil, Oger, 51190 Avize
Tel: 26 57 52 43

History. Founded in 1922 by Ferdinand Bonnet and run
by the third generation under Mlle Nicole Bonnet until
1988, when the House and its vineyards were acquired by
Charles Heidsieck.

Visiting:	By appointment
Vineyards:	10 ha in Oger and Avize (Ch), and Vertus (PN)
Annual Prod:	140-160,000 bottles
Exports:	30% mostly to the UK

House Style:	*Chardonnay*-influenced, delicate, light with balance and finesse.

Crémant Brut NV (90% Ch, 10% PN)
Fine flowery nose with hint of ageing. Light and delicate
with a good finish.

Vintage Sélection Blanc de Blancs (100% Ch)
Very floral nose, light and delicate. Belies the fact that
their vintage wines are aged for up to seven years.

Other wines include *Blanc de Blancs Réserve Brut* (100%
Ch), and *Carte Blanche,* (a Ch/PN blend).

BRICOUT

Ancien Château d'Avize, 59 Rue de Cramant, 51190 Avize
Tel: 26 57 53 93

History. Until quite recently this House was known as Bricout-Koch and this reflected its strong German roots. In 1820 Charles Koch from Heidelberg established his champagne House in Avize, more than fifty years before the House of Bricout was founded in Epernay by Arthur Bricout. In 1869 Bricout, then employed by Champagne de Venoge, married Constance Kupferberg, daughter of Christian Kupferberg , who had created a prosperous *Sekt* House in Germany. The two Houses merged when Bricout moved to Avize, and the House of Bricout-Koch was created, based in the Château d'Avize.

Their fortunes fluctuated until 1966 when Andréas Kupferberg, the great-grandson of Charles, joined the House. By 1979 the House, by then wholly owned by Kupferberg, was taken over by the Racke Group, and a period of rapid expansion took place. Wineries have been m odernised, and the champagne is now sold under the name Bricout.

Visiting:	By appointment
Vineyards:	About 4 ha.
Annual Prod:	2.8 million bottles
Exports:	25-30%
House Style:	Straightforward, fruity, easy-drinking wines with elegance from *chardonnay*, always at least 40% of the blend.

Carte Noire Brut Réserve (40% Ch, 35% PN, 25% PM)
Golden colour, vigorous *mousse*, fruity, youthful wines. Perhaps a little too young due to new cool fermentation techniques.

Carte d'Or Brut Réserve (55% Ch, 45% PN)
Mature, classy wine with good ripe fruit. Rich and complex with a big finish, has longevity.

Elégance de Bricout 1985 (60% Ch, 40% PN)
Very pale, lemony colour but big in body, depth and flavour. A very classy wine which will go on improving.

Rosé Brut (80% Ch, 20% PN)
Very lightly coloured, slightly light on fruit and heavy on
acidity but lively, crisp and refreshing, good finish.

Millésime Brut 1985 (60% PN, 40% Ch)
A substantial wine with rich fruit but good balance.
Classy, easy-drinking, good long finish.

ALBERT LE BRUN

**93 Avenue de Paris, 51000 Châlons-sur-Marne
Tel: 26 68 18 68**

History. Founded in Avize in 1860 by Léon le Brun and still a family-run firm, although now based in Châlons with modern facilities and huge cellars.

Visiting:	By appointment
Vineyards:	4 ha.
Annual Prod:	About 350,000 bottles.
Exports:	55%.

House Style:	Very well-made, traditional wines, big, rich and great value.

NV Blanc de Blancs Brut (100% Ch)
Almost smoky bouquet, big, rich and ripe, mature fruit. Great value.

NV Cuvée Réservée Brut (65% PN 35% Ch)
The *pinot* influence comes through but biscuity and fruity with a long finish.

Vintage Cuvée Réservée Brut (40-50% PN, 50-60% Ch)
Another big, rich, mature wine with lots of fruit and good balance. Long finish.

Vintage Vieille France Brut (55% PN, 45% Ch)
The House's flagship wine although the blend and quality varies. Can lack balance.

There is also a *Carte Blanche Brut*, *Demi-Sec* and *Rosé Brut*.

CANARD-DÛCHENE

1 Rue Edmond Canard, 51500 Ludes
Tel: 26 61 10 96

History. Founded in 1868 by Victor-François Canard, this *grande marque* House did not really start to grow until the 1930s when production topped 300,000 bottles. By the 1950s sales had reached 500,000 bottles a year and production was stepped up reaching more than 2.2 million bottles in 1980. In 1973 Piper-Heidsieck bought one third of the company's shares but sold this holding to Veuve Clicquot who acquired the House in 1978. The House now has very modern winery facilities and more than 2 kilometres of cellars.

Visiting:	Open daily May-September. Appointments needed to visit cellars.
Vineyards:	17 ha in Ludes and Taissy.
Annual Prod:	3 million bottles.
Exports:	10-15%.
House Style:	Good value, well-made, elegant, characterful wines.

NV Brut (33% Ch, 33% PN, 33% PM)
Almost always very good value, elegant and flowery, rich, mouth-filling flavour.

Cuvée Speciale Charles V11 Brut (66.6% Ch, 33.3% PN)
The House's prestige wine. Golden yellow with strong, persistent *mousse*. Hints of hazelnuts and tropical fruits, good balance and long finish.

Vintage Brut (33% Ch, 33% PN, 33% PM)
Pale gold in colour, medium-bodied, rich, mature fruit. Quality can vary.

DE CASTELLANE

**57 Rue de Verdun, 51200 Epernay
Tel: 26 55 15 33**

History. De Castellane is one of the oldest families in
France, and it was Vicomte Florens de Castellane who
founded the house in Epernay in 1895. He chose the
famous St. André Cross, in red, which was the banner of
Champagne's oldest regiment, for his very distinctive
label.

Fernand Mérand was responsible for the move into the
House's current spectacular premises. The house, with 10
kilometres of cellars, was built in 1904 by Auguste
Marius Toudoire, the architect of the Gare de Lyon in
Paris. Fernand's son Alexandre bought the company in
1936.

By the early 1950s, de Castellane had become one of
the largest champagne Houses. Hervé Augustin,
Alexandre Mérand's grandson, took over the company in
1984 and has been responsible for its growth since then.
Exports have quadrupled over the last seven years and are
expected to top 1 million bottles a year by the end of
1992. Laurent Perrier acquired a twenty per cent share of
the company in 1984 and now have a controlling interest.

Visiting:	Daily May-September 1000-1130 and 1400-1700.
Vineyards:	None.
Annual Prod:	3.3 million bottles.
Exports:	30%.

House Style: Soft, light, well-made, easy drinking wines. Good value.

NV Brut Croix Rouge de Saint André (30% Ch, 30% PM, 40% PN)
Slight smokiness in the nose. Fine, well-rounded and fruity, with *chardonnay* flavours coming through gently. Good value.

Vintage Brut Croix Saint André 1986 (40% Ch, 53% PN, 7% PM)
Very pleasant nose with hints of *brioche*. Fresh and fruity to taste. Well-balanced, with a long finish.

Rosé Croix Rouge de Saint André Brut (44% Ch, 43% reserve wines from red and white crus, 13% red wine from Bouzy)
Light and fruity nose. Bigger, rounded fruit in the mouth but still light and well-balanced.

NV Brut Blanc de Blancs (100% Ch)
Made from the best *crus* from the Côte des Blancs. Persistent, delicate *mousse*, light but firm fruit and long lingering finish.

Vintage Cuvée Royale Chardonnay (100% Ch)
Only made in exceptional years with wines from Cramant, Oger and Mesnil-sur-Oger. Very fine, subtle, spicy nose. Rouded, creamy, classic *blanc de blancs,* with long and full finish.

Cuvée Commodore 1986 (60% PN, 40% Ch)
A fine wine with complex, intense nose – toasted almonds and nougat. Big and rounded on the mouth, well-balanced and with a long, lingering finish.

Cuvée Florens de Castellane 1982 (100% Ch)
Fine, flowery nose. Well-balanced and rounded in the mouth. Much finesse.

CATTIER

6 Rue Dom Pérignon, Chigny-les-Roses,
51500 Rilly-la-Montagne
Tel: 26 03 42 11

History. A family-owned House founded at the turn of
the century, although they have owned vineyards at
Chigny-les-Roses for more than 200 years. A traditional
producer using vats for maturation and producing top-
quality wines.

Visiting:	By appointment.
Vineyards:	20 ha.
Annual Prod:	250,000 bottles.
Exports:	30-35%, mainly to UK and US.

House Style:	Big, rich, full-bodied wines with good balance.

NV Brut (50% PN, 50% Ch)
Fruity, hazelnut nose. Big up-front wine with lots of fruit
and acidity but good balance.

Vintage Brut (50% PN, 50% Ch)
Pleasant nose with nougat and fruit tones. Big and fruity
in the mouth, but well-balanced.

Clos du Moulin Brut (50% Ch, 50% PN)
Very good wine with complex fruits and flavours on the
palate. Hints of quince. Delicate, with long, lingering
finish.

DE CAZANOVE

1 Rue des Cotelles, 51205 Epernay
Tel: 26 54 23 46

History. Founded in Avize in 1811 by Charles Gabriel de Cazanove, the House specialised from its earliest days in using the lighter, more delicate wines of the Marne. The House was sold to the Moët-Hennessy group in 1979 and was acquired by S.A.M.E. in 1985, under the control of the Lombard family.

Visiting:	By appointment only.
Vineyards:	None.
Annual Prod:	1.9 million bottles.
Exports:	40%.
House Style:	Generally *pinot*-dominant blends, to produce firm, rounded wines with good balance and depth of fruit. Good value.

NV Brut (70-80% PN, 20-30% Ch)
Predominantly *pinot* blend to give a big, rounded wine with fine, persistent *mousse*. Attractive young, fresh grapey, yeasty nose. Well-balanced rich fruit on the palate and a long finish.

NV Rosé Brut (70-80% PN, 20-30% Ch)
A very fruity *rosé*, with good colour and soft, fruity nose. Good, ripe, curranty fruit flavours with depth and balance. A lingering finish.

Ruban Azur Brut (80% Ch, 20% PN)
A very elegant wine with firm, persistent *mousse* and creamy, floral nose with vanilla aromas. Good rounded fruit on the palate with a long crisp finish.

Vintage Brut 1985 (70-80% PN, 20-30% Ch)
An attractive wine with good *pinot* nose and ripe red fruit aromas. Lashings of ripe fruit on the palate, with a long, strong finish.

Champagne Stradivarius. Tête de Cuvée, Brut 1985 (70% Ch, 30% PN)
Soft golden colour with fine, creamy, persistent *mousse*. A soft, biscuity, nutty nose with ripe red fruit aromas, and full, rich fruit on the palate. Great balance and a long, lingering finish.

A. CHARBAUT & FILS

17 Avenue de Champagne, 51205 Epernay
Tel: 26 54 37 55

History. The family has been in the champagne business for more than 150 years, although it was not until 1948 that the House was founded by André Charbaut. He was born at Fère-Champenoise and worked in a brewery, before learning his trade in Champagne working as Commercial Director for the House of Ducoin in Mareuil-sur-Aÿ for some twenty-eight years.

Charbaut now owns impressive cellars in Epernay which date back to the 1700s, and storehouses and reserve cellars in Mareuil-sur-Aÿ. The House also owns a pressing station at Mareuil where it crushes its own grapes, and those of other *vignerons*.

The family business is run by André's sons, René and Guy Charbaut, and son-in-law Jean-Pierre Abien. The House has grown considerably in the past few years and does a lot of own-label bottling for hotels and restaurants. In the early 1960s the House acquired the firm of Ducoin, and a period of major expansion followed. It supplies champagne to Sainsbury's, and its De Courcy label is popular in the UK. The House moved to its present

offices on the prestigious Avenue de Champagne in 1893.
There are 4 kilometres of nineteenth-century cellars but
new, more functional cellars have now been built.

Visiting:	Open weekdays except Wednesday. Groups by appointment only.
Vineyards:	56 ha, all in the *grand cru* areas of Mareuil-sur-Aÿ, de Bisseuil, D'Avernay-Val-d'Or, and Viviers-sur-Artaut. (10 ha Ch, 46 ha PN).
Annual Prod:	1.5 million bottles.
Exports:	50%, especially to the UK and US.
House Style:	The House specialises in *blanc de blancs* and *rosé*. Well-produced, attractive wines with good fruit and character.

CHAMPAGNE

A. CHARBAUT ᴇᴛ FILS

BRUT

EPERNAY
(FRANCE)

750 ml

PRODUCT OF FRANCE
Alc.12% by vol

NM·145·001

NV Brut (33% Ch, 67% PN)
Spends at least three years on its lees in the bottle before
disgorgement. Very flowery, apple-fruity bouquet. Clean,
crisp, rich fruit in the mouth. Well-balanced and good
finish.

NV Brut Rosé (10% Ch, 90% PN)
The grapes are left to macerate with their skins for thirty-
six hours which results in the very delicate salmon-pink

colour. Attractive berry fruit and peaches on the nose.
Medium- to full-bodied but elegant. Good acidity
balancing rich berry fruit with hints of raspberries. Good
value.

NV Blanc de Blancs (100% Ch)
Spends at least four years on its lees before disgorgement.
Perfumed, slightly spicy nose. Light and elegant, with
good fruit, and long, crisp finish.

NV Cuvée de Réserve Brut (33% Ch, 67% PN)
Very complex and elegant with toasty, *brioche* bouquet
and hints of vanilla. Firm fruit, but good balance and long
finish.

Vintage 1985 Brut (33% Ch, 67% PN)
Produced only in exceptional years. Aged separately and
left to settle for four years before being disgorged.
Aromas of lemon, peach and apples. Elegant and well-
balanced. Rich, complex fruit flavours. Also
recommended – 1982, 1979.

Le Certificat Blanc de Blancs 1985 (100% Ch)
Also only produced in outstanding years. Powerful
bouquet of fruits and flowers, apples and vanilla.
Chardonnay, buttery, spicy elegance with good, mouth-
filling fruit. Full of flavour, and long, lingering finish.
Also recommended – 1982, 1979.

A. CHAUVET

11 Avenue de Champagne, 51150 Tours-sur-Marne
Tel: 26 59 92 37

History. Founded in 1848, this small family House owns 10 hectares of vineyards which provide almost all its needs.

Visiting:	Weekends by appointment.
Vineyards:	10 ha (4 ha at Ambonnay, Bouzy, Verzenay and Verzy, and 6 ha at Bisseuil).
Annual Prod:	55,000 bottles.
Exports:	10-15%.
House Style:	High quality, very distinctive wines. Excellent with food.

NV Brut (60% PN, 40% Ch)
Good balance between *pinot* fruit and vigour, and *chardonnay* elegance. Good fruit and long crisp finish.

NV Blanc de Blancs (100% Ch)
Mouth-filling, creamy and fruity. Very drinkable.

NV Grand Crémant Rosé (predominantly PN blend)
Gentle but vigorous *mousse*, with a firm, spicy nose and big ripe fruit on the palate . Very good with food.

Vintage Brut (50% PN, 50% Ch)
Very well made with great balance. Mouth-filling and long, lingering finish.

Vintage Crémant Rosé (blend n/a)
A very distinctive style with powerful nose. Big and gutsy to taste. More than a match for many strongly-flavoured dishes.

COLLERY

2 Place de la Libération, 51180 Aÿ
Tel: 26 54 01 20

History. A wine-making House with a long tradition in
Champagne. Records show that the family, which has
always been based in Aÿ, was supplying grapes to the
abbey of Hautvillers long before Dom Pérignon arrived
on the scene. In the mid-1890s the family started to
produce its own wines. The House is now run by Alain
Collery.

Visiting:	Cellars and museum open daily for visitors.
Vineyards:	9 ha – 7 ha at Aÿ and 2 ha at Mareuil-sur-Aÿ.
Annual Prod:	80,000 bottles.
Exports:	35%.
House Style:	Wines with great fruit but matched by finesse and elegance. Characterised by the typical Aÿ bouquet.

NV Réserve Brut (80-90% PN/PM, 10-20% Ch)
Lovely soft, ripe-fruit nose and big fruit flavours bursting
on the palate. Well-balanced, with depth and a long
finish.

NV Réserve Rosé Brut (100% PN)
Soft, ripe-berry, fruit aromas on the nose and creamy, rich
fruit flavours on the palate. Well-structured with good
balance and depth. A long, lingering finish.

Cuvée Solange Collery (100% PN)
A *blanc de noir* using only black grapes from the House's
Aÿ vineyards. A new label, launched in 1989. A very
elegant wine, with a very attractive creamy, soft, red-fruit
nose. Well-balanced fruit on the palate which lingers
through to the end in a long, strong finish.

DELAMOTTE PERE & FILS

5 Rue de la Brêche d'Oger, 51190 Mesnil-sur-Oger
Tel: 26 57 51 65

History. The House was founded by François Delamotte in 1760 and started trading under the name of Delamotte Père & Fils in 1786 when his two sons, Alexandre and Nicholas-Louis, joined the firm. When Alexandre died in 1828, his brother joined forces with Jean-Baptiste Lanson, and changed the name of the House to Louis Delamotte Père & Fils. In 1837 Lanson's nephews Henri and Victor-Marie also joined the company, and the name was changed yet again to Veuve Delamotte-Barrachin. Twenty years later, the Lanson family acquired full control of the House and changed the name to Lanson Père & Fils, although the Delamotte name was still used on many of the wines. In the early 1920s the Delamotte *marque* was bought by Marie-Louise de Nonancourt, sister of Victor and Henri Lanson, and in 1927 the House of Delamotte Père & Fils was resurrected in Mesnil-sur-Oger.

Visiting:	By appointment.
Vineyards:	None.
Annual Prod:	180,000 bottles.
Exports:	40-50%.
House Style:	Youthful wines with good fruit and balance that benefit from further ageing.

NV Brut (PN/Ch blend n/a) Attractive creamy fruit on the nose and palate. A pleasant wine but lacks depth and finish. Needs more time to come together. There is also a *sec* and *demi-sec.*

Vintage Brut (PN/Ch blend n/a) Good, ripe fruit on nose and palate. Well balanced with some depth. Good finish.

Blanc de Blancs (100% Ch) A youthful wine which will improve further with a little more ageing. Attractive nose with yeasty, fruity aromas and good body and depth of fruit on the palate. Needs time to round off some of the edges.

Rosé Brut (PN/Ch blend n/a) A soft, easy-drinking rosé, with fine, creamy *mousse*, and good ripe *pinot* fruit on the nose. Very fruity on the palate with good depth and balance, and a clean, crisp finish.

A. DESMOULINS

44 Avenue Foch, 51201 Epernay
Tel: 26 54 24 24

History. Founded in 1908 by Albert Desmoulins, and still run by the family as a tiny company devoted to producing small-volume but high-quality wines.

Visiting:	By appointment.
Vineyards:	None.
Annual Prod:	150,000 bottles.
Exports:	15%.
House Style:	Very good value, flavourful wines of good balance and depth.

NV Cuvée de Réserve Brut (50% PN/PM, 50% Ch)
A very good NV wine better than many vintages from other Houses. Classy and elegant, with a very fine, persistent *mousse*. Complex, flowery, fruity nose and full-flavoured on the palate with good depth and balance. A long, lingering and clean finish.

There are also a *sec* and a *demi-sec* made from the same blend.

Grand Rosé Brut (blend n/a)
Very elegant on nose and palate. Soft, creamy ripe-berry fruit aromas and flavours. Good, ripe, lingering fruit on the palate and a good finish.

NV Cuvée Prestige Brut (50% PN/PM, 50% Ch)
Golden yellow with flashes of green and with a firm, persistent *mousse*. Nose is light with lots of fresh fruit aromas, and these develop well on the palate. Good balance, well-rounded and with a firm finish.

Vintage Blanc de Blancs 1982 (100% Ch)
Very appealing soft, creamy, fruity nose. Good biscuity and fruit flavours on the palate, and an attractive hint of sweetness. Good finish.

Brut Idéal (blend n/a)
A no-*dosage* wine of great finesse and balance. Delicate white-gold colour. Soft, attractive nose with yeasty, *brioche* aromas. Great balance and depth in the mouth, with a long, lingering finish.

DE TELMONT

1 Avenue de Champagne, 51480 Damery
Tel: 26 58 40 33

History. The House was founded in 1920, but the De
Telmont family have been making wines in the
Champagne region for many generations. They have
earned a reputation for producing the highest quality
champagnes because of their careful selection of grapes,
their adherence to traditional wine-making techniques
(even though they have a very modern winery), and their
large stocks of reserve wines.

Visiting:	By appointment.
Vineyards:	At Damery
Annual Prod:	800,000 bottles.
Exports:	30%.

House Style:	Delicate, light wines with suppleness and good fruit. Good value.

NV Grand Réserve Brut (PN/PM/Ch blend)
A good value non-vintage with body, depth and balance.
Vigorous *mousse* and clean, fresh and fruity on the nose.
Good balance and a long, lingering finish. There is also a
sec.

Grand Vintage Brut 1983 (blend n/a)
A wine of great refinement and balance. Fine persistent
mousse and complex, soft, ripe, fruit aromas. Firm and
full-bodied on the palate with good, ripe fruit and a long,
crisp finish.

Blanc de Blancs Brut (100% Ch)
A very elegant, light-bodied wine with great charm.
Good, soft, rounded fruit on nose and palate. Long finish.

Grand Rosé Brut (100% PN)
A gloriously-coloured, medium-bodied rosé with soft,
ripe, red fruit on the nose and rich fruit flavours in the
mouth. Good balance and depth, and a long, clean finish.

Cuvée Grand Couronnement (100% Ch)
A lovely wine with complex nose and flavours. Higher
than usual proportions of reserve wines give great depth
and balance. A big, satisfying wine of class.

DEUTZ

16 Rue Jeanson, BP No. 9, 51160 Aÿ
Tel: 26 55 15 11

History. The House was founded in Aÿ in 1838 by
William Deutz and Pierre-Hubert Gelderman, who both
came from Prussian Aachen – then French-controlled and
called Aix-La-Chapelle. Gelderman had worked as a
salesman for Bollinger, while William Deutz ran his own
négociant business. Gelderman's son Alfred then married
William's daughter Marie, to cement the union between
the two families.

Between 1868 and 1896 sales trebled to 600,000 bottles
a year and Deutz became a *grande marque*.

On 11 April, 1911 the Deutz offices, and most of the
vineyards and stocks, were destroyed in the 'Champagne
Riots'. It took the company almost twenty years to
recover, although it expanded considerably as it did so.
Five generations on, it is still an independent family-run
company under André Lallier-Deutz. All vinification is
still done by traditional methods. The House owns a
major *Sekt* producer in Germany and a Californian
vineyard, and is involved in joint ventures in Argentina
and South Korea.

Visiting:	By appointment, with an introduction from an agent.

Vineyards:	42 ha (14 ha Ch at Mesnil-sur-Oger, and 28 ha PN, mostly at Aÿ and Mareuil).
Annual Prod:	900,000 bottles.
Exports:	55%.
House Style:	Fresh, fruity, youthful wines with power and depth, finesse and length.

NV Brut (55% PN, 20% PM, 25%Ch)
A blend of three or four vintages, producing a very pleasant, grassy, refreshing wine. Very pleasing lemony hints on the palate.

Vintage Brut 1985 (60% PN, 15% PM, 25% Ch)
Very concentrated nose, elegant fruit and good balance, considerable finesse, long finish.

Vintage Blanc de Blancs 1985 (100% Ch)
A big nose but not heavy. Very soft, creamy and fruity on the palate. Hints of *brioche*. Very elegant.

Vintage Rosé Brut 1985 (100% PN)
The grapes come from the famous *crus* of Aÿ, Ambonnay, Verzenay and Bouzy. Very light in colour because of the addition of only a small quantity of Bouzy wine. Good *pinot* fruit on the nose, and crisp and firm on the palate. Good, long finish.

Cuvée William Deutz 1985 (62% PN, 30% Ch, 8% PM)
Named in memory of the founder of the House and only

made in exceptional years (1971, 1975, 1979, 1982, 1985). Very traditional *cuvée* and aged for between five and eight years before it is released. Wonderful nose full of perfumes and aromas, and bursting with ripe fruit on the palate. Long-lasting, great balance and good value.

Réserve Cuvée Georges Mathieu (33% Ch, 67% PN/ PM) Wonderful wine, wonderfully presented in packaging created by the artist after whom it is named. Hints of hazelnuts and peaches on the nose, and lashings of fresh, ripe fruit on the palate. A big but elegant wine with long, long finish.

DOYARD ET FILS

61 Avenue de Bammental, 51130 Vertus
Tel: 26 52 14 74

History. The House of Robert Doyard was founded in
1927, although the family has been based in Vertus and
making wines for many gener ations. Its wines were
previously sold through brokers who marketed them
under different names. Maurice Doyard was one of the
founders of the *Comité Interprofessionnel du Vin de
Champagne* in the spring of 1941. The company is still
family-owned.

Visiting:	By appointment.
Vineyards:	At Vertus (93% Ch, 7% PN)
Annual Prod:	50,000 bottles.
Exports:	30%.

House Style:	Light, characterful wines with freshness, fruit and flavour.

NV Brut Reserve
A fresh, lively wine with attractive soft nose and rich,
ripe fruit on the palate. A good, clean finish.

NV Rosé
Medium- to full-bodied *rosé* with attractive red fruit and
hints of toast and vanilla on the nose. Clean, well-
balanced fruit on the palate. A lingering finish.

Vintage Brut 1985
Medium- to full-bodied but very fresh and full-flavoured.
Very attractive, complex nose with floral, soft red fruit,
toasty aromas. Good balance and depth, and a long, clean
finish.

Cuvée Spéciale Extra-Brut
A big, classy wine, with lashings of rich, ripe fruit on
nose and palate. Good balance, depth and complexity, and
a long, lingering finish.

DRAPPIER

Grande Rue, F-10200 Urville
Tel: 26 27 40 15

History. The Drappier family can trace their roots in
Champagne back to 1604; to Remy Drappier who was a
draper in Reims. One of his descendants, a Maître Nicolas
Drappier, was Procurator to Louis X1V. During the reign
of Napoleon 1, the family moved to Urville to cultivate
their own vineyard and produce wine. The *domaine* and
House have been run by the family ever since. The House
has extensive cellars under Reims which were dug out
from the chalk during the last century, as well as twelfth-
century cellars constructed by the monks of Clairvaux, at
Urville. These cellars hold the special and rare
champagnes.

Visiting:	Monday-Saturday, 8 am-12 noon and 2-5 pm.
Vineyards:	27 ha (15% Ch, 15% PM, 70% PN).
Annual Prod:	600,000 bottles.
Exports.	50%, the UK being the main overseas market.
House Style:	Big aromatic wines, rich and fruity, stylish, and capable of great longevity. Good value.

NV Cuvée Carte d'Or Brut (85% PN, 10% PM, 5% Ch)
Typical of the House style, clean, big, rich and fruity.
Well-balanced, with lots of flavour from *pinot* fruit and a
big, long dry finish.

Vintage Cuvée Carte d'Or Brut 1988 (50% Ch 50% PN)
Well-made, complex wine, toasty bouquet. Big, elegant
and complex on the palate, with a long and creamy finish.

NV Cuvée Blanc de Blancs Signature (100% Ch)
Vigorous, creamy *mousse*, elegant, toasted nose, rich, ripe
chardonnay fruit.

NV Rosé Brut 'Val des Demoiselles' (100% PN)
Named after the small *pinot noir* vineyard which
produces the grapes for this very elegant, intense wine.
Fine, creamy *mousse*, raspberry, slightly spicy nose.
Strong, aromatic and good *pinot* fruit on the palate. Good

balance and a long finish.

Grande Sendrée Brut 1985 (55% Ch, 45% PN)
Named after an old vineyard, planted more than seventy
years ago, which produces exceptional vintages and
outstanding wines. Highly fragrant bouquet of spicy
vanilla and citrus flavours. Full of creamy flavour on the
palate with a long, dry lingering finish. A great wine and
very good value.

DUVAL-LEROY

Rue du Mont Chenil, 51130 Vertus, BP 37
Tel: 26 52 10 75

History. The House was founded in 1859 when the two firms of Jules Duval and Edouard Leroy were merged. The Duval family took the management and still control the company today. The House has a substantial 'own-label' business. It is one of the leading exporters to the UK, albeit anonymously as most of the wine appears under the labels of major supermarket chains and wine merchants.

Visiting:	By appointment.
Vineyards:	About 100 ha mostly in the best areas of the Côte des Blancs.
Annual Prod:	Over 4 million bottles.
Exports:	15-20%.
House Style:	Well-made, good-value wines, with full fruit flavour and good balance.

NV Rosé Brut (70-80% Ch 20-30% PN)
Unusual in that it has only a short maceration which gives it a striking orange-pink colour. Very light and elegant, lots of fruit but good balance. Quaffable.

Vintage Brut (33% Ch, 33% PN, 33% PM)
Strong, attractive nose with *pinot* berry fruits and *chardonnay* floral elegance. A big wine in the mouth.

NV Fleur de Champagne Brut (75% Ch, 25% PN)
Elegant, lots of rich fruit and floweriness on the palate. Good value.

NV Cuvée des Roys Brut (90% Ch 10% PN)
Very elegant, but with great depth from extra ageing. Harmonious, with a long, long finish.

There are also *NV Demi-Sec* and *Fleur de Champagne Demi-Sec*.

ELLNER

1 Rue Côte Legris, 51200 Epernay
Tel: 26 55 60 25

History. The House was founded at the beginning of this century by Charles-Emile Ellner, who immediately started to purchase small high-quality vineyard plots as they came on the market. His son Pierre expanded their vineyard holdings and promoted their product abroad. The company is still family-owned and each of his four sons has specific responsibility for a different activity – vineyards, wine-making, management or marketing.

Visiting:	By appointment.
Vineyards:	52.24 ha (42.8% Ch, 28.8% PN, 28.4% PM) in 15 villages.
Annual Prod:	500,000 bottles.
Exports:	50%.
House Style:	Elegant, well-structured wines with balance and good rounded fruit.

Cuvée de Réserve (60% Ch, 40% PN)
Very elegant wine with fine, persistent *mousse*. Attractive nose with soft ripe fruit and vanilla, and toasty aromas. Good depth of fruit on the palate, well-balanced, with a long finish.

Carte d'Or (90% Ch, 10% PN)
Very delicate but persistent *mousse* and a soft, creamy, ripe fruit nose with vanilla edges. Light and elegant on the palate with good depth and a long, lingering finish.

Rosé Brut (50% PN, 50% PM)
Fruity and easy-drinking. Attractive ripe, red fruit nose and full flavoured on the palate, with sustained, clean finish.

Blanc de Blancs (100% Ch)
Elegant wine with very fine, persistent *mousse*. Soft, creamy ripe berry nose with toasty, nutty and vanilla aromas. Rich, ripe fruit on the palate with good depth and balance, and a long, lingering, fruity finish.

Crémant Blanc de Blancs (100% Ch)
Very attractive, soft, easy-drinking wine. Soft and creamy

on the nose and palate, with good fruit and acid balance. A good rounded finish.

Prestige Millesime 1985 (70% Ch, 30% PN)
Full bodied but still very light and elegant. A very fine, persistent *mousse*. Good, complex nose with ripe red fruit bouquet and hints of vanilla, nuts and *brioche*. Good rounded fruit on the palate with depth and balance, and a long, clean, crisp finish.

Vintage Brut 1985 (75% Ch, 25% PN)
An attractive nose with soft berry fruit aromas, and big, rich, almost honeyed fruit on the palate. A big wine, well structured with a long finish.

Qualité Extra Brut 1982 (50% PM, 20% PN, 30% Ch)
A big wine with rich, ripe fruity flavours and quite a strong taste of citrus. A crisp, refreshing wine with quite high acidity.

NICOLAS FEUILLATTE

BP 210, Chouilly, 51206 Epernay
Tel: 26 54 50 60

History. Nicolas Feuillatte, a Champagne grower, created his own label about twenty years ago, and continues to travel the world promoting his champagne. Due to increasing success world-wide, and in order to guarantee supplies for his wine, M. Feuillatte entered into an agreement with the *Centre Vinicole de la Champagne* (CVC) in 1986. This means that a large number of producers have a ready-made market for their quality wines, and the growers' group is now one of the most powerful in Champagne. Each year, members of the CVC, which is based near Epernay, bring the juice from their 1,250 ha of vineyards to the company for vinification.

Visiting:	Monday to Friday. Guided tours at 10 am, 2 pm and 4 pm. Groups of more than 8 should book at least eight days in advance.
Vineyards:	Grapes are bought from members comprising the Nicolas Feuillatte Company, who between them own 1,250 ha of vineyards – about a quarter of the total champagne area.
Annual Prod:	15 million bottles.
Annual sales:	1.5 million bottles.
Stock:	40 million bottles.
Exports:	40%
House Style:	Mature wines with complexity. Full of fruity, floral flavours with balance and suppleness.

Blanc de Blancs Brut Premier Cru (100% Ch)
Pale straw colour with tints of green, fine delicate *mousse*.
Fresh, elegant nose and creamy, fruity taste. Long,
complex and well-balanced.

Rosé Brut Premier Cru (60% PN, 30% PM, 10% Ch plus
addition of red wine)
A pretty salmon colour, with fine, persistent *mousse*. Fruit
nose with aromas of ripe cherries, strawberries and
currants. Fresh and mouth-filling with a long finish.

Réserve Particulière Brut Premier Cru (50% PN, 30% PM, 20% Ch)
Colour of gold straw. Fine, vigorous *mousse*, with a flowery, fruity nose with hints of spices. Firm but supple on the palate, well-balanced and with a long finish.

Vintage 1982 Brut Premier Cru (50% PN, 25% PM, 25% Ch)
Pale yellow, with vigorous, persistent *mousse*. Buttery, complex nose with hints of *brioche*, apple and quince. Well-balanced with good length.

Cuvée Spéciale Palmes d'Or 1983, Brut Premier Cru (40% Ch, 40% PN, 20% PM)
Pale yellow golden colour with fine, persistent *mousse*. Flowery nose with strong apple and pear aromas. Big, mouth-filling fruit, but good balance and long, strong finish.

Also produced are *Ratafia*, one of the oldest aperitif drinks of Champagne, and *Bouzy Rouge*.

ROLAND FLINIAUX

1 Rue Léon Bourgeois, 51160 Aÿ
Tel: 26 55 17 17

History. The House was founded in 1938, although the family have been involved in champagne as *vignerons* since 1905, when Joseph Fliniaux bought the prestigious Les Rocherets vineyard, close to Epernay. The cellars and their stocks of champagne were destroyed by bombing in 1944. The company relocated in Aÿ and is now famous for its unmistakable Aÿ-style wines.

Visiting:	Weekdays 9 am to 12 noon and 2-6 pm.
Vineyards:	4 ha in the Vallée de la Marne.
Production:	100,000 bottles.
Exports:	15%.
House Style:	Heady, almost overpowering wines. Very well made, with good balance, and full of rich fruit aromas and flavours. Good value.

NV Carte Bleue Brut (80% PN, 20% Ch)
A great big wine, bursting with rich, ripe fruit but well
balanced and with a long, strong finish.

NV Rosé Brut (100% PN)
A big wine and a very good rosé. Creamy, strawberry
flavours on the nose, and rich fruit flavours in the mouth,
with a firm, lingering finish. Good value.

Vintage Carte Noire Brut (100% PN)
Fine, vigorous *mousse* and attractive nose. Well made
with good fruit and balance. Needs a little ageing.

There are also *NV Carte Rouge Brut* (80% PN, 20% Ch) and *NV Carte Noire Brut* (80% PN, 20% Ch).

GARDET

13 Rue Georges-Legros, 51500 Chigny-les-Roses
Tel: 26 03 42 03

History. A small, family-owned House, founded in 1895 in Chigny-les-Roses. The House sticks faithfully to traditional methods of wine-making and has a higher than usual production of vintage wines, which are aged rather longer than those from many other Houses. The modern winery replaced buildings destroyed by Allied bombing because of their unfortunate proximity to a German V2 rocket site.

Visiting:	By appointment.
Vineyards:	None.
Annual Prod:	600,000 bottles.
Exports:	20%.

House Style:	Wines of elegance and maturity, well balanced with good fruit and flavour and very good value.

NV Brut Spécial (70% PN, 30% Ch)
Soft, ripe fruit nose and rich, creamy, full fruit flavours on the palate. Good balance and depth and a long finish.

NV Rosé Brut (100% PN)
A big, medium- to full-bodied rosé with soft, red fruit and currant aromas and creamy, rich fruit on the palate. A classy rosé with depth and character, and a long, stylish finish.

Vintage Brut (50% PN, 50% Ch)
Classy and mature with great balance, depth and complexity. Big, rich, mouth-filling wine.

RENÉ GEOFFROY

150 Rue des Bois des Jots-Cumiéres,
51480 Cumieres
Tel: 26 55 32 31

History. A very traditional House which can trace its
roots in Champagne and wine-making back to the
beginning of the seventeenth century. It concentrates on
small volume production of the highest quality, using
traditional wine-making methods.

Visiting:	By appointment.
Vineyards:	12 ha (20% Ch,38% PM, 42% PN) at Cumières, Hautvillers and Damery.
Annual Prod:	100,000 bottles.
Exports:	10%.
House Style:	Wines that need a little longer to mature than most, because malolactic fermentation is not used, but they develop well and can have great longevity.

NV Cuvée de Réserve Brut (90-95% PN/PM, 5-10% Ch)
Usually a blend of two vintages and a wine of remarkable
complexity. Very fine vigorous *mousse* and soft, fruit
aromas on the nose with hints of spices and ginger. Very
fresh, ripe-fruit flavours in the mouth and a long finish.

NV Rosé Brut (PN/PM blend)
A medium-bodied wine, fresh, fruity and elegant. Good
ripe red fruit on the nose and rich, rounded fruit on the
palate. Good depth and balance with a long, lingering
finish.

Vintage Cuvée Sélectionnée 1982 (66%PN, 34% Ch)
A very elegant wine with massive, complex nose packed
with attractive aromas – floral, fruity, toasty, nutty, vanilla
and oak. Intense fruit flavours on the palate and a long,
sustained, clean finish. A wine that will improve further
with ageing.

Vintage Cuvée Prestige 1985 (66% Ch, 34% PN)
A very classy wine with great longevity. Fine, persistent
mousse with rich rounded fruit and firm acid on the palate.
Already drinking well but will improve further with
ageing.

The House also produces the excellent *Cumières Rouge*, a
pure *pinot noir* red wine, fermented in small oak barrels
and blended from three different vintages.

H. GERMAIN

31 Rue de Reims, 51500 Rilly-la-Montagne
Tel: 26 03 40 19

History. Founded in 1898 by Henri-Antoine Germain, and now marketing under the Germain and Binet labels. Germain is particularly popular in the United States. The Binet *marque* was established in Reims in 1849 and was acquired from Piper-Heidsieck during the Second World War.

Visiting:	Visitors welcome.
Vineyards:	48 ha of PN, PM and Ch.
Annual Prod:	1.3 million bottles.
Exports:	30%.
House Style:	Very dry wines with intense bouquets and elegance.

NV Carte Blanche Brut (50% PN, 35% PM, 15% Ch)
A fine, persistent *mousse* and a rich, almost honeyed nose with soft, fruit aromas. Full, rich fruit flavours in the mouth with some depth. Well-balanced with a good finish.

NV Rosé Brut (95% PN/PM, 5% Ch)
A light, elegant wine, although dark pink in colour. A soft, fruity nose with good red fruit flavours on the balance, although the finish is a little abrupt.

Vintage Carte d'Or Brut 1983 (25% Ch, 60% PN, 15% PM)
A persistent *mousse* and attractive, complex nose with toasty, smoky aromas. Full-flavoured in the mouth with rich, ripe fruit. Good balance and depth and a long finish.

Blanc de Blancs Brut 1983 (100% Ch)
A big, rich full-bodied *blanc de blancs* with elegance. An attractive, intense nose of soft, crea my fruit aromas and lively, rich fruit flavours on the palate.

PAUL GOBILLARD

Château de Pierry, Pierry, 51200 Epernay
Tel: 26 54 05 11

History. The House was established in 1941 and
restructured in 1972, although the family has a longer
vine-growing tradition in Champagne, with Paul
Gobillard owning vineyards in Pierry in the late
nineteenth century.

Visiting:	By appointment.
Vineyards:	A small vineyard in Pierry producing *pinot meunier*.
Annual Prod:	150,000-200,000 bottles.
Exports:	5-10%
House Style:	Elegant, fruity wines because higher proportions of *pinot meunier* are generally preferred.

NV Carte Blanche (25% Ch, 25% PN, 50% PM)
A very attractive, very fruity wine because of the *pinot
meunier* influence. Fine, delicate *mousse* with great
persistence. Soft, floral nose and full, rich fruit on the
palate. Good balance with acidity and a long, lingering
finish.
A *sec* and a *demi-sec* are made from the same blend.

Blanc de Blancs (100% Ch)
Elegant and delicate, with a fine, persistent *mousse* and a
soft, flowery nose with vanilla aromas. Good ripe fruit on
the palate and crisp acidity for balance. Attractive, with a
long finish.

NV Cuvée Régence (50% Ch, 50% PN/PM)
Bottled in an eighteenth-century-style flagon, the wine is
both big and delicate. It has a very attractive nose with soft,
ripe red fruit aromas and lots of full-flavoured fruit on the
palate. Good balance and depth, with a good firm finish.

Vintage Brut 1982 (66% Ch, 34% PN/PM)
A very elegant wine with a delicate *mousse* and a big, rich
nose full of red fruit and ripe berry aromas. Equally full
and generous on the palate, with ripe fruit and good
balancing acidity which will mellow further with ageing. A
long, lingering finish.

MICHEL GONET

**196 Avenue Jean Jaurès, 51190 Avize
Tel: 26 57 50 56.**

History. The House was founded in 1802. One of the
great strengths of the company is its vineyard holding
which was built up over several generations. The
company also has extensive vineyards in Bordeaux.

Visiting:	By appointment.
Vineyards:	40 ha spread over the most prestigious villages (80% Ch).
Annual Prod:	400,000 bottles.
Exports:	80%

House Style:	Light, elegant wines with heady bouquets and fresh fruit.

NV Brut Réserve (50% PN, 50% Ch)
A big wine with good balance and depth. It has a fine,
vigorous *mousse* and an attractive, ripe-red fruit nose with
aromas of berries. Big, lively fruit on the palate, good
balance and a long, lingering finish.

NV Rosé Brut (100% PN)
A stunning reddish-pink wine with a powerful, ripe-red
fruit nose. It is lively and fresh on the palate, with good,
lasting fruit and a long, lingering finish. Goes very well
with food.

Vintage Blanc de Blancs Grand Cru 1982 (100% Ch)
A very good *blanc de blancs* with a fine, persistent
mousse and a soft, creamy nose full of fresh, youthful
fruit. The fruit flavours open up on the palate and linger
on right to the end. Very attractive.

GOSSET

69 Rue Jules Blondeau, BP 7, 51160 Aÿ
Tel: 26 55 14 18

History. One of the smallest champagne Houses but by
far the oldest. Founded in Aÿ in 1584 by Pierre Gosset,
the House has been selling wines for the last 400 years –
long before champagne was invented in the mid-
eighteenth century. The present directors of the company
are direct descendants of the founders, and are the
thirteenth and fourteenth generations of the Gosset
family.

The wines are made traditionally, and there is no
malolactic fermentation, which the family believes
accelerates the ageing process too quickly – it does not
result in the same quality or taste of a traditional, slowly-
aged champagne. Wines that have undergone malolactic
fermentation do not remain in optimum condition as long,
and lose their freshness more quickly.

The House holds large stocks of champagne –
equivalent to five years sales – in order to maintain the
quality and balance of its prestige *cuvées*. In the early
1970s it sold most of its vineyards to Krug, and in 1980 it
acquired the champagne House of Philipponnat, selling it
seven years later to the spirits company Marie Brizzard.

Visiting:	None.
Vineyards:	12 ha of PN (about 10% of its needs) in Aÿ, Mareuil-sur-Aÿ, Bouzy and Rilly-la-Montagne. Additional grapes are only bought from Marne vineyards.
Annual Prod:	850,000 bottles.
Exports:	37%
House Style:	Traditional. Always a combination of black and white grapes to produce full-bodied, rich, creamy and toasty wines with complexity and maturity.

NV Brut Réserve (55% Ch, 38% PN, 7% PM)
A blend of eight top *cru* villages. Versatile, medium-
bodied wine with good balance and depth. More ageing
than many NV wines, and it shows. Long, full finish.

NV Rosé (67% Ch, 23% PN, plus still red wine from PN, from Aÿ and Bouzy)
Delicate, pale, salmon colour. Full, soft and fruity, lingering finish. In 1947 Gosset became the first House to use a clear glass bottle for *rosé* champagne, to show off its colour to the best advantage.

NV Grand Réserve (48% Ch, 40% PN, 12% PM)
A very upmarket elegant *cuvée*. A big, harmonious wine, rich and full of complex flavours. Good value.

Vintage 1985 Brut (36% Ch, 58% PN, 6% PM)
A complex blend of *premier cru* wines from twenty villages. A big wine with aromatic *pinot* nose and *chardonnay* elegance. Good rich fruit in the mouth, but still fresh and youthful. Well-balanced, with a strong finish.

Vintage 1983 Brut (47% Ch, 53% PN)
Aged for seven years, and it shows. Full-bodied, with great balance and finesse. Still surprisingly fresh on the palate with lashings of fruit. Great with food.

Vintage Rosé 1985 Brut (100% Ch)
Pale rose colour and a light, delicate bouquet. Fresh, light and fruity on the palate with elegance.

ALFRED GRATIEN

30 Rue Maurice Cerveaux, BP 3, 51201 Epernay
Tel: 26 54 38 20

History. The House was founded in 1864 in Epernay by 23-year-old Alfred Gratien, who established at the same time a company in Saumur which still produces quality sparkling wines. In the 1870s Jean Meyer joined the firm, which today has the title Gratien, Meyer and Seydoux, and is run by Eric Seydoux, his two sons Alain and Gérard, and his cousin Bernard de Bousquet. All are direct descendants of the founders.

For five generations the House has remained faithful to traditional methods of production. This explains why, when sales of all champagne more than doubled between 1965 and 1978, the production of Champagne Alfred Gratien increased only slightly. Only the best grapes from the Marne are used and all efforts are concentrated on producing just three wines – a vintage and a non-vintage *brut* – and a *rosé*. The House is believed to be one of the few still using oak casks for the first fermentation, and the only one still using a *conche* – a blending through the first floor of the winery from which casks are fed by gravity alone.

Visiting:	By appointment, weekdays 9 am-12 noon and 2-6 pm.
Vineyards:	None.
Annual Prod:	180,000 bottles.
Exports:	80%.
House Style:	Traditional, with lots of *pinot meunier* fruit coming through in the NV wines.

Mature, full-bodied and consistent, good value.

NV Brut (44.5% Ch,5.9% PN,49.55% PM)
Full-flavoured, classy, mature champagne. Fine, vigorous *mousse* and yeasty, biscuity nose. Very attractive fruit on the palate with slight pepperiness. Very good value.

NV Rosé (30% Ch, 10% PN, 60% PM)
Lovely orangey-pink colour. Fine, delicate *mousse* and very attractive, toasty, fruity nose. Rich, creamy, fruity and full of grape flavour. Very well-balanced, soft but firm, with a long lingering finish. Will improve further with age.

Vintage 1983 Brut (61% Ch, 33.5% PN, 5.5% PM)
A big, glorious wine. Delicate, flowery bouquet, but full-bodied and classy. Lashings of rich, ripe fruit and toasty flavours. Wines of longevity which will go on improving if kept. Also recommended are the 1982 and 1979.

HAMM

**Maison Emile Hamm et Fils, 16 Rue Nicolas Philipponnat, 51160 Aÿ
Tel: 26 55 44 19**

History. The House was founded in Aÿ in 1930 by Emile Hamm. He was born in Mareuil in 1885, although his family were originally from Alsace. The House moved to its present premises in 1942 and the firm is now run by Claude Hamm.

Visiting:	Monday to Friday 8 am to 12 noon and 2-6 pm. Weekends and Bank Holidays 9 am-12 noon.
Vineyards:	4 ha in Aÿ.
Annual Prod:	250,000 bottles.
Exports:	20%.
House Style:	Elegant, fruity wines. Good value. Particularly popular in Switzerland.

NV Sélection Brut (50% PN, 50% Ch)
Fine persistent *mousse* and good soft fruit nose with toasty, vanilla aromas. Good, fresh *pinot* fruit on the palate with good depth and balance, and a long finish.

NV Réserve Grand Cru Brut (60% PN, 40% Ch)
Medium- to full-bodied, but still fresh and elegant. Vigorous *mousse* and attractive ripe, red fruit on the nose. Full-flavoured on the palate, with a sustained, clean finish.

NV Rosé Brut (60% PN, 40% Ch)
Medium- to full-bodied and very fruity. Soft, creamy, rich fruit on the nose, very full-flavoured on the palate but with elegance and depth. Good, fruity finish.

Vintage Brut 1985 (50% Ch, 50% PN)
Very good balance and depth. Attractive nose with floral, fruity aromas and hints of nuts and vanilla. Big and full-flavoured on the palate. A long, lingering, clean finish.

CHARLES HEIDSIECK

3 Place des Droits-de-l'Homme, 51055 Reims
Tel: 26 40 16 13

History. The House was founded in 1785 by German-born Florenz-Louis (originally Florenz-Ludwig) Heidsieck, although it was not until 1851 that the name Charles Heidsieck was used and became established as a *marque*. Despite the popularity of the Heidsieck name in champagne, none of the Houses using it today are connected, although they derive their origins from a common ancestry. Today they all operate as separate companies.

In 1845, Charles-Camille Heidsieck, son of one of the founder's nephews, joined the champagne House of Piper, which was run by his aunt. In 1851 he married Amélie Henriot, and left Piper to join his brother-in-law Ernest at the House of Henriot. Together they created a new champagne which was marketed under the Heidsieck name, and the House was founded. It was Charles who was responsible for promoting the champagne in the United States, which he loved to visit because of all the hunting. He quickly earned the affectionate nickname of 'Champagne Charley' in the US but spent a short time in jail in 1861, after being arrested by the Yankees during the Civil War. He was caught carrying a diplomatic bag containing contracts from French clothing manufacturers to supply the Confederate army. The courier mission was not the main purpose for his trip, however, because he was really trying to reach New Orleans in order to recover a large debt.

Members of the family have always been ambassadors for their wines and have been largely responsible for their success on the international market, especially in Britain and Ireland.

In 1976 the House was acquired by Henriot and in 1985 Charles Heisieck was sold to Rémy Martin. The House is a *grande marque*, and has huge chalk cellars, for storing and slow ageing, thirty metres below ground. These were excavated by the Romans 2,000 years ago.

Visiting:	By appointment.
Vineyards:	Almost none.
Annual Prod:	3 million bottles.
Exports:	70%.

House Style:	Very approachable, light and soft with good rich fruit and roundness.

NV Brut Réserve (38% PN, 37% PM, 25% Ch)

An *assemblage* of massive proportions involving more than 300 different elements – *crus*, grape varieties and reserve wines. Quite a high proportion of the blend comes from reserve wines, and it shows. The wine has a brilliant golden colour, with a complex bouquet of different floral, ripe fruit and toasty aromas and a hint of vanilla. It is a big, smooth, well-balanced wine with lashings of ripe fruit and a long, lingering finish.

Vintage Brut 1985 (60% PN, 5% PM, 35% Ch)

A creamy, biscuity nose with almost chocolatey aromas. Full-bodied, round, rich fruit flavours on the palate and a long finish.

Rosé Brut 1985 (60% PN, 8% PM, 32% Ch)

An appealing light-pink colour with fine but persistent *mousse*. A delicate, fresh nose, with soft, rich fruit on the palate. Great balance and depth, and a long, lingering finish.

Blanc des Millénaires 1983 (100% Ch)

Produced in limited quantities and only in exceptional years. Selected grapes from five of the top *Côte de Blancs* vineyards are used to produce this wine, which is pale golden in colour, with a very fine but persistent *mousse*. It has a marvellous youthful, fresh, flowery nose with aromas of violets, and nutty, toasty, honeyed undertones. The wine grows in the mouth, developing in complexity with nutty, fruity flavours, strong hints of wood and candied peel, but all very well balanced, and elegant. A long finish and a very good wine.

HEIDSIECK ET CIE MONOPOLE

83 Rue Coquebert, 51000 Reims
Tel: 26 07 39 34

History. The company traces its roots back to the firm founded by Florenz-Louis Heidsieck in 1785. In 1834 the House was founded in its own right when one of Florenz-Louis's nephews, Henri-Louis Walbaum, established his own company called Walbaum – Heidsieck. The brand name of Monopole was created around the middle of the nineteenth century, and the House was widely known as Heidsieck Monopole, although this was not officially incorporated into the firm's name until 1923. Until then it had been a family-controlled business, but in that year it was acquired by the supermarket chain Comtoirs Français, who used the new name to differentiate their Heidsieck House from the others.

In 1972 the House was acquired by the Seagram drinks empire though its champagne subsidiary Mumm. They own extensive vineyards, including one at Verzenay. This is overlooked by a massive windmill, bought by the company in 1923, and now used as a hospitality centre and observation post. The windmill, the Moulin de Verzenay, was built in 1823 and is one of the most famous landmarks of the Montagne de Reims.

Visiting:	None.
Vineyards:	110 ha – 21 ha at Verzenay, 21 ha at Ambonnay, 19 ha at Verzy, 3 ha at Bouzy, 2½ ha at Mailly and Beaumont-sur-Vesle – all PN, 22.5 ha at Faverolles-Chardonnay, and 21 ha at Savigny-sur-Ardre – PM.
Annual Prod:	1.5 million bottles.
Exports:	60%
House Style:	Quality wines of richness and elegance with great balance.

NV Dry Monopole Brut (73% PN/PM, 27% Ch)
A fine, persistent *mousse* and an attractive nose with soft, concentrated fruit. The fruit opens out on the palate to give a long finish. Well made and well balanced. Good value.

NV Monopole Red Top Sec (73% PN/PM, 27% Ch)
Medium dry taste with good fruit and underlying acidity
for balance. Long finish. Good with sweets.

NV Monopole Green Top Demi-Sec (73% PN/PM, 27%
Ch)
Very sweet but not cloying. Long finish

Dry Monopole Brut Vintage (42% Ch, 58% PN/PM)
A big wine with rich, ripe *pinot* aromas on the nose and
full fruit flavour on the palate. Good acidity for balance,
and a long finish.

Dry Monopole Rosé Vintage (42% Ch, 58% PN/PM)
Elegance from the *chardonnay* but soft, fresh *pinot* fruit
dominates attractively on nose and palate. Well-balanced,
mature wine with elegance.

Diamant Bleu Vintage (50% Ch, 50% PN/PM)
The cuvée spéciale of the House and made only with
grapes from 100% *cru* vineyards. A wine of great finesse
and complexity. A very fine but persistent *mousse*, soft
fruit aromas on the nose with traces of *brioche* and
vanilla, and exceptional balance on the palate. Rich,
rounded and long lasting.

HENRIOT

4 Blvd Henri Vasnier, 51100 Reims
Tel: 26 82 63 22

History. Archives show that the Henriot family moved to
the Champagne region in 1640, settling in Reims. In 1791
Nicolas Henriot purchased the Customs and Royal Farms
House in Place Royale, Reims. It became the headquarters
for their varied businesses, principally vine growers and
wool merchants. Accounts dated 1807 show they were
also producing their own wines.

It was not until the mid-nineteenth century, however,
that the fame of their wines grew internationally, and in
1850 they received a Royal Warrant from the King of
Holland. A year later Amélie Henriot, who was married to
Charles Heidsieck, persuaded her brother Ernest to join
forces with Charles and sell their champagne under the
Charles Heidsieck label. It was a disastrous liaison, and
much of the company's land and assets had to be sold to
pay Charles's debts. There were further financial disasters,
including a ruinous project planting vineyards in Russian
Turkestan. By 1918 the vineyards were derelict, the cellars
had caved in and the mansion in the Place Royale had
burnt down.

The fame of the Henriot label, however, lived on and
this persuaded Etienne Henriot to re-create and extend the
vineyards. Today the firm has 110 hectares of vines, all in
the most famous areas, and it still adheres to the traditional
methods of wine making. Since 1808 it has cultivated its
special style, based on the belief that the fame of its brand
is due entirely to the quality of its *cuvées*. Nothing must be
done to undermine this, and the firm believes that 'time is
our ally, and patience our secret.' The wines are aged in
four hectares of chalk cellars, excavated by the Romans
2,000 years ago in the centre of Reims.

Ironically, Henriot bought back Charles Heidsieck in
1976 but it was sold again in 1985, when Veuve Clicquot
acquired the Henriot name. It continues, however, to live
its own life.

Visiting:	By appointment only.
Vineyards:	110 ha (65% Ch, 35% PN), in the Montagne de Reims, Vallée de la Marne and Côte des Blancs.

Annual Prod:	1 million bottles.
Exports:	40%.

House Style:	Great character and elegance because of predominance of top-*cru chardonnays*.

NV Souverain Brut (60% PN, 40% Ch)
Bone dry with strong *chardonnay* characteristics on nose and palate. Elegant but with pronounced fruit. Good balance and long, dry finish.

NV Blanc de Blancs Brut (100% Ch)
Lively and skittish, with a fine but persistent *mousse*. Very floral nose. Light and fruity, fresh and elegant. Long, attractive finish with tangs of citrus.

Vintage 1985 Brut (60% PN, 40% Ch)
Big wine which needs time to develop fully. Complex and characterful. Fine but vigorous *mousse*, powerful nose of apples, spices and touches of vanilla. Fruity and lively on the palate, with great length and balance. Long strong, almost spicy finish.

Vintage Rosé Brut (predominantly Ch with addition of red wine made from PN)
Only made in exceptional years. Delicate pink colour, vigorous *mousse*. Elegant and light, with subtle nose and palate.

Cuvée Baccarat, Vintage 1982 Brut (55% Ch, 45% PN)
A blend from fifteen prestigious *crus* to produce a complex, elegant, aromatic wine. Yellow-gold in colour with a fine but persistent *mousse*, and very floral nose with hints of almonds and spices. Delicate on the palate but good balance and a long, lingering finish.

INVERNAL

4 Rue Jules-Lobet, 51100 Aÿ
Tel: 26 50 11 00

History. The House was founded in 1963 by Bernard
Invernal, but the family can trace its history in the
Champagne region back to the 1500s. There was another
Invernal House founded towards the end of the last
century, but it did not trade for very long. Bernard's
father, Henri, was *chef de cave* at both Krug and Louis
Roederer. Invernal wines are very popular in France and
listed by many top restaurants.

Visiting:	By appointment.
Vineyards:	2 ha at Aÿ (PN and PM).
Annual Prod:	250,000 bottles.
Exports:	35%
House Style:	Attractive, rich wines, well-balanced, well made.

NV Réserve Brut (40% Ch, 60% PN/PM)
Easy-drinking with good fruit, but higher than usual
dosage level prevents this from being a really dry wine. Its
sweetness is in no way unpleasant and comes across well
in a rich, fruity, clean finish.

NV Rosé (40% Ch, 60% PN/PM)
Medium-bodied with fine, vigorous *mousse* and lots of
rich, ripe fruit on the nose and palate. Good balance and
depth, and a satisfying finish.

Cuvée du Roi François 1 (50% Ch, 50% PN/PM)
An easy-drinking wine of very good balance and depth.
Very fine, vigorous *mousse*. Attractive nose with floral,
fruity aromas and hints of vanilla and *brioche*. Good,
balanced fruit on the palate and a clean, crisp finish.

NV Blanc de Blancs (100% Ch)
A very easy-to-drink wine with fine, persistent *mousse* and
soft, creamy, fruity nose with vanilla and toasty aromas.
Good, rich, mouth-filling fruit and a long, lingering finish.

Vintage Brut (50% Ch, 50% PN)
Pale golden colour with very fine, persistent *mousse* and
attractive, complex nose. Full-bodied and rounded on the
palate, with good balance and depth, and a long, clean
finish.

JACQUART

5 Rue Gosset, 51066 Reims
Tel: 26 07 20 20

History. The House was founded in 1962, when thirty of the top grape producers in Champagne – all concerned about preserving the qualities of their own individual vineyards – got together to launch their own champagne blend. The *Coopérative Régionale des Vins de Champagne* was created and Champagne Jacquart was launched. The company is one of the few selling its own branded wines direct to the public, and likes to call itself 'the youngest of the major champagne Houses'. In their first year they produced just 100,000 bottles from 20 hectares of vineyards.

In 1968 the House purchased its own building and constructed three floors of arched champagne cellars out of the chalk hillsides of Reims. Four years later, as the company expanded and more growers joined, the House moved to its present headquarters in Rue Gosset. In 1981 it launched its flying horse trademark and started to develop its export trade.

The cooperative's members own extensive vineyard holdings and produce about 10 million bottles of champagne a year, of which about a quarter is marketed under the Jacquart label, and the rest as Buyers' Own Brands. They also own more than 1,000 hectares of vineyards and their operation makes them the sixth largest champagne producer. During the harvest, 155 presses located throughout the Champagne region work day and nigh t to press the grapes and ensure their freshness. Only the first pressing is used for Champagne Jacquart.

Visiting:	Trade only, by appointment.
Vineyards:	About 1,000 ha in the Vallée de la Marne, Montagne de Reims and Côte des Blancs.
Annual Prod:	10 million bottles.
Exports:	35%.
House Style:	Overriding balance and freshness, with lively fresh fruit and rich, yeasty flavours. Medium- to full-bodied.

Brut Tradition (33% PN, 33% PM, 33% Ch)
The most popular Jacquart style, with fruit, body and
elegance. Very typical of the new-style, lighter
champagnes.

Brut Selection (50% Ch, 35% PN, 15% PM)
Very light and elegant because of the *chardonnay*
influence, but with good structure and body, courtesy of
the *pinot noir*, and roundness, thanks to the *pinot
meunier*. Brilliant, light golden colour with fine but
persistent *mousse*. A soft, creamy, fruity nose with hints
of *chardonnay*-inspired vanilla. Creamy in the mouth,
with nutty, yeasty flavours and good balancing acidity. A
long, strong finish.

Brut Rosé (50% Ch, 35% PN, 15% PM)
A very rich rosé with attractive coral-pink colour, and a
soft, peristent *mousse*. A soft, fruity, almost spicy nose
with big, rich, ripe fruit on the palate. Rounded and well-
balanced with a long finish.

Vintage Brut 1985 (50% Ch, 50% PN)
Only produced in exceptional years and left on the yeast
for at least five years, to produce wines of great
complexity and character. A very delicate, perfumed
nose. Crisp, rich and full of ripe fruit on the palate. Great
balance and a long, lingering finish.

Cuvée Nominée Blanc 1985 (60% PN, 40% Ch)
Produced only in exceptional years, and only from grapes
from the finest vineyards. The wine spends at least five
and a half years on the yeast, for added complexity. It is
full-bodied, with creamy, toasty, fruit flavours on the
palate and firm acidity for excellent balance. A long, long
finish.

Cuvée Nominée Rosé 1985 (60% PN, 40% Ch, then plus
15% PN wine from Bouzy)
The same *cépage* as the above, but with the addition of
red wine from Bouzy, it produces a wine of great
elegance and charm. A very attractive soft fruit and floral
nose, with big, rich fruit and toasty flavours on the palate,
and a long finish.

JACQUESSON & FILS

68 Rue du Colonel Fabien, 51200 Dizy
Tel: 26 55 68 11

History. The House was founded in 1798 by Claude Jacquesson and his son Memmie, at Châlons-sur-Marne. The ten kilometres of cellars so impressed Napoleon that he presented the House with a Gold Medal which still features on their labels. Memmie's son Adolphe expanded the firm, and his sister-in-law married Joseph Krug who was working for the company. In 1843 Krug left Jacquesson to set up his own House. By the 1860s the House was producing about 1 million bottles a year, more than double its current output. The concentration now is on quality rather than quantity.

Visiting:	Monday-Thursday, 8 am-12 noon and 1.30-5.30 pm, Friday, 8 am-12 noon and 1.30-4.30 pm.
Vineyards:	33 ha – 11 ha Avize (Ch), 3 ha Dizy Hautvillers (Ch), 1 ha Aÿ (PN), 4 ha Dizy Hautvillers (PN), 4 ha Dizy Hautvillers (PM), 2 ha Vallée de l'Ardre (PN), and 8 ha Vallée de l'Ardre (PM).
Annual Prod:	400,000 bottles.
Exports:	45%.
House Style:	Classy but very approachable wines. Soft, easy to drink and very good value.

NV Perfection Brut (20% Ch, 30% PN, 50% PM)
Very floral and full-flavoured. Well-balanced, creamy, ripe fruit with a long elegant finish.

NV Blanc de Blancs Brut (100% Ch)
Very elegant, light, fresh and fruity with great finesse.

NV Perfection Rosé Brut (20% Ch, 40% PN, 30% PM plus 10% of red wine made from PN)
Lovely creamy, raspberry nose. Complex, well-balanced and long, soft finish.

Perfection 1985 Brut (35% Ch, 50% PN, 15% PM)
Complex and with great balance. Firm, vigorous *mousse*. Creamy, ripe fruit nose, and soft, rich fruit on the palate. Good value.

Signature 1983 (50% Ch, 50% PN)
Aged in oak casks giving attractive oaky flavours which
complement the rich fruit. A very classy wine with great
longevity.

Cuvée de Prestige 1975 Dégorgement Tardif (100% Ch)
A wine that was not disgorged until just before being
released from the cellars for sale. It has developed
tremendous complexity, while retaining an astonishing
freshness with massive, mouth-filling assorted fruit
flavours. Very fine but vigorous *mousse,* and a long, long,
memorable finish.

JEANMAIRE

12 Rue Godart Roger, BP 256, 51207 Epernay
Tel: 26 54 60 32

History. The House was founded in 1933 by André Jeanmaire, a young vineyard owner in Mesnil-sur-Oger, in the heart of the Côte des Blancs. He established himself as a champagne merchant, and started to produce and sell on a small scale. The company quickly outgrew its premises and, after World War II, moved to Epernay. The founder died in 1971, and the House passed to his daughter and son-in-law. They ran the business until 1982, when Michel Trouillard bought the company and its vineyards.

The House moved to its current address and is now one of the most modern in Champagne, although it still honours the traditional wine-making techniques of the region. The five kilometres of cellars were excavated at the end of the last century and reconstructed in 1981, when the winery equipment and machinery were fully modernised.

Visiting:	By appointment only.
Vineyards:	80 ha – 10 ha Avize, 8 ha Cramant, 12 ha Chouilly – all *chardonnay,* 8 ha Tauxiéres, 3 ha Les Mesneux, 3 ha Villedommange, 7.5 ha Orbais-l'Abbaye, 4.5 ha Reims, 5 ha Dizy, 7 ha Champillon and 12 ha others – all *pinot noir.*

Annual Prod:	1 million bottles.
Exports:	60%.
House Style:	Very elegant, fresh and light.

NV Brut (40% PN, 30% PM, 30% Ch)
A blend of at least thirty different wines, and aged for at least three years to let the aromas develop. Golden yellow colour with fine but vigorous *mousse*. Elegant, flowery nose, and fresh and balanced in the mouth.

NV Blanc de Blancs Brut (100% Ch)
A blend of ten different *chardonnay* and reserve wines, and aged for at least three years. Yellow with green tints, and a fine, persistent *mousse*. Elegant floral nose, and light, fresh fruity palate. Good finish.

NV Rosé Brut (70% PN, 30% PM)
Dark pink colour, as a result of *macération carbonique*, with a delicate, persistent *mousse*. A very powerful nose, full of red fruit aromas. Fresh and fruity on the palate, with a long, lingering finish.

Vintage Rosé 1985 (100% PN)
A blend of several *pinot noir grand cru cuvées*, vinified as *rosé* and aged for at least four years. Brilliant onion skin-colour, fine but persistent *mousse*, and delicate, red fruit flavours on the palate. Will improve with a little ageing.

Vintage Brut 1985 (55% PN, 35% Ch, 10% PM),
Yellow-gold in colour, with fine, persistent *mousse*. Very
complex nose, full of flowery, fruity aromas. Fresh and
youthful on the palate, with complex fruit, good balance
and a long finish.

Vintage Blanc de Noirs 1985 (85% PN, 15% PM)
Tiny but vigorous *mousse*, big nose with lots of fruit, and
full fruit flavoured in the mouth. Elegant, with a long,
lingering finish.

Vintage Blanc de Blancs Brut 1982 (100% Ch)
Aged for at least seven years. A golden-yellow colour and
with a fine but persistent *mousse*. Very elegant on nose
and palate, with freshness, complexity and a long finish.

Elysée 1976 (100% Ch)
Despite its age, an incredibly fresh and lively wine. Full,
aromatic *chardonnay* nose, great finesse and length.

KRUG

5 Rue Coquebert, 51100 Reims
Tel: 26 88 24 24

History. The House was founded in 1843 by Johann-Joseph Krug, who learned his blending skills while working at Jacquesson. He was born in Mainz in 1840, and changed his name to Jean-Joseph when he started working in Champagne in 1834. In 1841 he married Adolphe Jacquesson's English sister-in-law, Emma Anne Jaunay, at the British Embassy in Paris, and two years later, in partnership with Hippolyte de Vives, he started his own House in Reims.

He developed the 'Krug Taste', which is still maintained today by Henri and Rémi Krug, who represent the fifth generation of champagne makers. The founder wrote down the rules for creating a perfect champagne, and these are still adhered to today. Paul Krug took over the firm on the death of his father in 1866, and his eldest son, Joseph Krug II, succeeded him in 1910.

In 1914 he joined the French Army, but was wounded and taken prisoner in 1915. In his absence, his wife controlled the company, but Joseph returned at the end of the war so ill that he persuaded his nephew, Jean Seydoux, to join the firm in 1924. Joseph was told he did not have long to live and, as his son Paul was only six years old, the idea was that Jean would run the company until the son could assume control. In the event, Joseph lived until he was 98 years old. He handed the company over to Paul Krug II in 1959, and outlived Jean Seydoux, who died in 1962, by five years.

In the early 1970s vineyards were acquired in Aÿ and Mesnil-sur-Oger with the help of financial backing from Rémy Martin. The new vineyards provide the wines for the House's very successful *grand cuvée.*

Tradition is still the keynote of Krug's wine-making. The different wines to be used in the blend, and the proportions of each, are still under the personal control of the members of the family and not entrusted to anyone else. The grapes for pressing are still selected by hand and less juice is extracted to produce only the very best *vin de cuvée.* Oak barrels are still used for the first fermentation, all the bottles are *remué* by hand, and ageing is still the key to the champagne's distinction. Krug was chosen by the British royal family to celebrate the weddings of both the Prince and Princess of Wales, and the Duke and Duchess of York.

Visiting:	Monday to Friday, by appointment only.
Vineyards:	15 ha – 9 ha Aÿ (PN), 6 ha Le Mesnil-sur-Oger (Ch, including 1.87 ha Clos-du-Mesnil).
Annual Prod:	500,000 bottles.
Exports:	80%.
House Style:	Strong adherence to traditional methods. All the wines are fermented in oak barrels to produce wines of great complexity, balance and depth. All need time to mature and have great longevity.

NV Grand Cuvée (45-55% PN, 15-20% PM, 25-35% Ch) The flagship of the Krug family representing 80% of total production. It is a 'multi-vintage' *cuvée* of between six and ten different years, a blend of up to fifty wines from six to ten vintages. This gives great complexity and balance, and a very recognisable style. It is elegant and full of rich fruit with a long, firm finish.

NV Rosé Brut (5-10% PN, partially fermented on the skins, 45-50% PN traditionally fermented, 20-25% PM, 20-25% Ch)
A very delicate pale pink, with fine but persistent *mousse*. Elegant, flowery nose and full of soft, well-balanced fruit on the palate with a long, dry finish. A wine of great finesse.

Vintage 1982 Brut (54% PN, 16% PM, 30% Ch)
A big, full-bodied wine with complexity, depth and longevity. Produced from twenty-seven different crops, it has remarkable ripeness and character.

Recommended previous vintages: 1981, 1979 and 1976.
Older vintages are still drinking gloriously.

Clos du Mesnil (100% Ch)
Produced only from *chardonnay* grapes grown in a
walled vineyard dating back to 1698. It was acquired by
Krug in 1971, and they produced the first Clos du Mesnil
in 1979. Because of the very small production, the oak
barrels are taken to the vineyard, which is less than two
hectares in size, where the first fermentation of grapes
takes place. A rare, elegant wine of great finesse. Every
bottle is dated and numbered.

Krug Collection 1973
A wine of enormous complexity and longevity, with
heady aromas and bursting with mouth-filling fruit,
although remarkably fine and fresh. A small stock of wine
is retained from each vintage and laid down in the cellars
where it is stored over many years under perfect
conditions. These bottles form the Krug Collection and
they are released from time to time, in tiny quantities,
always as the very last bottles available of any particular
Krug vintage.

LANG BIÉMONT

Les Ormissets, Oiry, 51200 Epernay
Tel: 26 55 43 43

History. The House was founded in 1875 in Avize by
Henri Langd and although it has built up a substantial
export market in Europe and North Africa, its name is
still not well known. The House has a preference for
chardonnay in its blend, using a much higher proportion
than most.

Visiting:	By appointment.
Vineyards:	3 ha.
Annual Prod:	500,000 bottles.
Exports:	60%.

House Style:	*Chardonnay* dominates the blends, giving elegance and roundness.

Cuvée Réserve Brut (70% Ch, 30% PM)
A fine, vigorous *mousse* with a powerful fruit nose. Soft,
ripe fruit on the palate. A wine of elegance and some
depth, with a long finish.

Cuvée Rosé Brut (50-60% Ch, 40-50% PN/PM).
Delicate but persistent *mousse* with soft, fruit nose and
big, rich, ripe fruit on the palate. Good balance and depth,
with a lingering finish.

Vintage Blanc de Blancs 1986 (100% Ch).
Still youthful, but elegant with complex bouquet full of
toasty, berry fruit and vanilla aromas. A big wine on the
palate with lashings of fresh, lively fruit and a long finish.

Vintage Blanc de Blancs 1985 Cuvée d'Exception (100%
Ch).
Very classy wine with fine, persistent *mousse* and soft,
creamy, fruity nose. A wine of great depth with good
balance, full of mouth-filling fruit and a long finish.

LANSON

12 Blvd Lundy, 51056 Reims
Tel: 26 40 36 26

History. The House, one of the oldest in Champagne, was founded in 1760 by François Delamotte and remained in the control of the Delamotte family for almost a hundred years. In 1828 Nicholas-Louis Delamotte, son of the founder, changed the name to Louis Delamotte Père & Fils. The House worked closely with Jean-Baptiste Lanson, a leading *négociant,* and when Nicholas-Louis died in 1837, the name of the House changed again to Veuve Delamotte-Barrachin and Lanson introduced his two nephews, Henri and Victor-Marie, into the company. Delamotte's widow, who had the controlling interest in the firm, died in 1855 and the House was taken over by Jean-Baptiste, who changed the name to Lanson Père & Fils. The early years were troubled by family squabbles and it was not until 1894, when Henri-Marie Lanson took sole control of the company, that a major expansion programme was initiated.

In the UK, the House has held the Royal Warrant from every monarch since Queen Victoria.

In the 1920s there was a period of acquisition and growth. New premises and cellars were acquired in Reims, and the vineyard acreage was expanded. This expansion was continued by Henri-Marie's son Victor throughout the 1930s, at a time when many other Houses were content simply to consolidate. As a result, in 1945 the company was able to take advantage of the sudden demand for champagne. It launched its Black Label non-vintage wine, and boosted sales at home and abroad. During the 1960s and 1970s it introduced temperature-controlled stainless steel vats and in 1983 embarked on a massive expansion of cellar capacity, to allow a total stockholding of 26 million bottles and almost 10 million litres of wine in vats.

In 1976 Lanson acquired the House of Masse, next door to its cellars. In 1970 the drinks firm Ricard acquired almost half of all the Lanson shares and throughout the decade other shares were bought, particularly by members of the Gardinier family, Pierre Lanson's in-laws. By 1979 the Gardiniers had a controlling interest in the House, and had also acquired Pommery. Suddenly, in 1983, they sold both the champagne Houses to the massive BSN food group which controls Lanson today – providing it with both financial support and enormous marketing expertise. The new *cuverie,* the most up-to-date in Champagne, was completed at the end of 1991. The disgorging line can handle 8,000 bottles an hour.

Visiting:	By appointment.
Vineyards:	208 ha – 43 ha Montagne de Reims (37 ha PN, 6 ha Ch) in Ambonnay, Bouzy, Verzy, Verzenay and Beaumont; 66 ha Côte des Blancs in Avize, Cramant, Oger, Oiry and Chouilly (all Ch); 65 ha (52 ha PN, 13 ha Ch) in the Vallée de la Marne at Dizy, Hautvillers, Mareuil-sur-Aÿ and Champillon; and 18 ha in the Aube. (The wines from the vineyards do not carry the Lanson label.) There are a further 16 ha as yet unplanted.
Annual Prod:	5 million bottles.
Exports:	60%.
House Style:	Traditional wines with great elegance. Very delicate *mousse,* soft floral bouquets and very rounded, balanced fruit on the palate.

NV Black Label Brut (40% Ch, 60% PN/PM)
Lively, with a fine, persistent *mousse* and attractive flowery, appley nose. Rich and rounded on the palate, masking the dryness. It has good depth and a long, lingering finish.

NV Sec (40% Ch, 60% PN/PM)
Very well-balanced with good acidity matching the sweetness. Attractive style with a long finish.

NV Ivory Label Demi-Sec (40% Ch, 60% PN/PM)
Soft and creamy, not overly sweet. A firm, vigorous *mousse* with rich, ripe *meunier* fruit coming through well on the palate. Sweet but not cloying, with a long, clean finish.

NV Rosé Brut (36% Ch, 64% PN)
A fine, persistent *mousse* and onion-skin colour which

comes from the addition of red wine from Lanson's Bouzy *pinot noir* vineyards. Fresh, lively and full of fruit, yet with good depth because of generous proportions of reserve wines which show through. Very approachable now but will improve further with a little ageing.

Vintage Brut 1985 (52% PN, 48% Ch)
Still very young, with a very fine, persistent *mousse* and soft, aromatic nose with hints of toast, hazelnuts and vanilla. Big, rich and rounded in the mouth, with a long, long finish. Will improve further with age.

Spécial Cuvée 225 Brut (55% Ch, 45% PN)
A special *cuvée* launched to celebrate the House's 225th anniversary. A wine of great elegance and finesse, with wonderful balance and a long, mouth-filling finish.

Noble Cuvée de Lanson 1981 (40% PN, 60% Ch)
A prestige *cuvée* of the finest wines from the finest vineyards. Elegant and expensive, with stunning light *chardonnay* fruit on the palate and great balance, depth and complexity. A very long finish.

GUY LARMANDIER

30 Rue du Général-Koenig, 51130 Vertus
Tel: 26 52 12 41

History. A small family-owned House which established its first vineyard in the Côte des Blancs in 1961 and has already established a good reputation. A fifth of production is exported – mostly to Europe, but also to the United States, Japan and the Far East.

Visiting:	By appointment.
Vineyards:	7 ha (Ch and PN).
Annual Prod:	65-70,000 bottles.
Exports:	25%.

House Style:	Very light, elegant wines. Fine bouquet and soft, rounded fruit.

NV Brut (Ch/PN blend)
Very delicate elegant wine, with very fine, persistent *mousse,* and soft, creamy, flowery nose. Good fruit on the palate. A wine of depth and length, with a long finish.

NV Blanc de Blancs Cramant Brut (100% Ch)
Very elegant, delicate wine. Fine, persistent *mousse* and a soft, floral nose with nutty, toasty aromas. Well-rounded, balanced fruit in the mouth and a good finish.

NV Rosé Brut Premier Cru (80% Ch, 20% PN)
A very attractive *rosé* with soft, ripe fruit nose and good red berry/currant aromas. Full, rounded fruit on the palate. Long, lingering finish.

Vintage Brut 1985 (50% PN, 50% Ch)
A wine of good depth and balance. A fine, persistent *mousse,* soft fruit on the nose with hints of vanilla and nutty aromas. Big, ripe fruit in the palate with good acidity and a long finish.

LARMANDIER-BERNIER

43 Rue du 28 Août, 51130 Vertus
Tel: 26 52 13 24

History. The House was founded in 1930 and is still a small family-owned company. It has just over nine hectares of family-owned vineyards, although it now has to purchase additional grapes because of increased production.

Visiting:	By appointment.
Vineyards:	9 ha at Cramant.
Annual Prod:	100-120,000 bottles.
Exports:	10%.

House Style:	Cramant *chardonnay* dominates, to produce elegant wines with very intense floral bouquets and good depth. Good value for money.

NV Premier Cru Brut (75% Ch, 25% PN)
Very dry wine with fine, steady *mousse* and intense, complex nose with nutty, toasty aromas. Good fruit on the palate, well-balanced and with a good finish.

NV Blanc de Blancs (100% Ch)
Very elegant. Fine but persistent *mousse,* and attractive nose of toasty, hazelnut aromas. Concentrated ripe fruit on the palate with good depth and structure. A lingering finish.

NV Rosé Brut (75% Ch, 25% PN, plus red wine from their *pinot* vineyards at Vertus)
A medium-bodied wine with steady *mousse.* Attractive, soft, ripe red fruit nose and good, firm, rich fruit on the palate.

Vintage Spécial Club Blanc de Blancs Brut (100% Ch)
Very classy and bursting with Cramant *chardonnay* aromas and flavours. Fine but persistent *mousse.* Soft, creamy nose with toast, yeasty and nutty aromas. Rounded ripe fruit on the palate. Good long finish.

LAURENT-PERRIER

Domqine de Tours-sur-Marne,
51150 Tours-sur-Marne
Tel: 26 58 91 22

History. The family started to produce champagne in 1812, when the House was founded by Eugène Laurent. He moved from Chigny-les Roses in the Montagne de Reims to a former abbey, dating back to the eleventh century, in Tours-sur-Marne, situated at the crossroads of the three great champagne regions. The family were traditionally coopers and it is said that they started to produce their own champagne because they were fed up with seeing someone else's wine in their barrels.

The founder's son, also named Eugène, married Mathilde Perrier, and on his death in 1887 the firm changed its name to Veuve Laurent-Perrier. Mathilde died in 1925 without an heir and in the late 1930s the Laurent-Perrier *marque* was bought by Marie-Louise de Nonancourt, sister of Victor and Henri Lanson. Her son Maurice, whom she wanted to run the company, died in a German prison camp, so her youngest son Bernard took over at the end of the war when he was demobbed. Although Bernard had no experience of the champagne trade he was a quick learner and a remarkable business-man. He developed new export markets, especially in Africa, and was responsible for a phenomenal increase in production.

Backed by a very capable team, he has made Laurent-Perrier one of the largest and most influential of the champagne Houses.

Visiting:	By appointment.
Vineyards:	80 ha (which account for just under 10% of total production)
Annual Prod:	7.5 million bottles.
Exports:	60%.
House Style:	Elegant wines with wonderful freshness and fruit.

NV Brut (35-40% Ch, 60-65% PN/PM)
Light golden in colour with a very fine, persistent *mousse*. The nose is fresh and fruity with appley aromas, and it is

big and powerful on the palate although still youthful
with rich, berry flavours. A good finish and will improve
further with a little age.

NV Ultra Brut (35-40% Ch, 60-65% PN/PM)
No *dosage,* very flowery and almost steely. Very long,
bone-dry finish.

NV Rosé Brut (100% PN)
Excellent wine. Good, ripe but classy *pinot* fruit on the
nose with soft strawberry aromas, and a gentle *mousse.*
Ripe, up-front fruit on the palate, great balance and a long
satisfying finish. It goes excellently with food.

Vintage Brut 1985 (PN/Ch blend)
Very elegant, with fine, persistent *mousse* and rich,
creamy, ripe *pinot* fruit and biscuity aromas on the nose.
Rich, almost sweet fruit on the palate and a long finish.
An attractive youthful wine for drinking now or leaving
for a while.

NV Grand Siècle (50% Ch, 50% PN)
Very classy wine produced from blending only the finest
grapes from the Montagne de Reims and Côte des Blancs.
It has an intense, complex nose full of floral, toasty
aromas, and mouth-filling, rich, ripe complex fruit.

Grand Siècle Alexandra Rosé Brut 1982 (blend n/a)
The first release of a new wine named to celebrate the
birth of Bernard's granddaugher. A marvellously elegant
rosé in the grand style with wonderful fruit and great
balance and depth. Rare and expensive.

Vintage Grand Siècle 1982 (100% Ch)
Youthful and elegant with fresh, rich *chardonnay* fruit on
the nose and palate. The delicate but mouth-filling fruit
gives a touch of sweetness on the palate so not too dry.
Long, lingering finish.

Vintage Millésime Rare 1976 (blend n/a)
A very classy wine produced in a tiny quantities,
therefore very expensive.

LECLERC-BRIANT

67 Rue de la Chaude Ruelle, BP 108,
51204 Epernay
Tel: 26 54 45 33

History. The family has been growing grapes in
Champagne since the seventeenth century and the House
was founded in 1872. The House has acquired about
thirty hectares of vineyards since then, spread between six
villages throughout the region.

The House is now run by Pascal Leclerc, the fifth
generation, who is a great publicist for champagne. He is
in the Guinness Book of Records for his world-record-
beating champagne pyramid which consisted of almost
10,500 champagne flutes, and stood more than seven and
a half metres high. The House owns thirty hectares of
vineyards, scattered through the Vallée de la Marne and
around Epernay. These give considerable choice when it
comes to blending.

Visiting:	By appointment.
Vineyards:	30 ha (50% PN, 30% Ch, 20% PM)
	The grapes are cultivated naturally with
	no chemical fertilisers used at any time.
	The House uses only grapes from its
	own estates.
Annual Prod:	250,000 bottles.
Exports:	45%.

House Style: Very elegant, aromatic wines. Light, fruity and balanced.

NV Blanc de Noirs Brut Extra (70% PN, 30% PM)
Attractive, perfumed, yeasty nose, with rich fruit and a touch of citrus on the palate. Well-balanced with a good, strong finish.

NV Cuvée de Réserve Brut (30% Ch, 70% PN)
Lively, fruity nose and good full fruit on the palate. Well-balanced, with a long, strong finish.

Club Spéciale Vintage Brut 1985 (50% PN, 50% Ch)
A big, full-bodied wine with rich, ripe fruit, yet still youthful. Well-balanced with a good finish. Also recommended – 1982, 1978.

Rosé Brut (100% PN)
Produced traditionally, and spends several days on its skin to give the wine its distinctive deep copper colour and rich fruity flavours of apples and berries, with a touch of spiciness. Good balance and depth, and a pleasing, lingering finish.

There is also a *demi-sec,* perfumed and fruity, well-balanced and ideal as a dessert wine.

Cuvée Mozart (75% PN, 25% Ch)
A prestige *cuvée.* Not tasted.

LEGRAS

**10 Rue des Partelaines, Chouilly, 51200 Epernay
Tel: 26 54 50 79**

History. Although vine-growers for many generations, it
was not until 1972 that René and Lucien Legras started
selling their own champagne. They concentrate on
producing small quantities of high-quality wines which
are listed, often as own label, by many top restaurants.

Visiting:	By appointment.
Vineyards:	22 ha in the Côte des Blancs and Montagne de Reims.
Annual Prod:	300,000 bottles.
Exports:	20%.
House Style:	Wines of great elegance and quality, made only from *chardonnay*.

Blanc de Blancs (100% Ch)
A very classy wine favoured by many of France's leading
restaurants. Very delicate, persistent *mousse* and soft, ripe
fruity nose with toasty, vanilla aromas. Elegant and
rounded on the palate with good depth of fruit, great
balance and a long, lingering, clean finish.

Cuvée St. Vincent (100% Ch)
A superior prestige *cuvée*. Very fine, persistent *mousse*
and soft, attractive, complex nose full of flowery, ripe
fruit aromas with hints of vanilla, toast and nuts. Big,
rich, ripe fruit bursts on the palate. A wine of great
balance and depth with a long, strong finish.

Brut Integral (100% Ch)
A no-*dosage* wine with great floweriness and soft ripe
fruit on the nose. Full, mouth-filling fresh fruit, great
depth and balance and a long, clean, very crisp finish.

LENOBLE

35 Rue Paul Douce, 51480 Damery
Tel: 26 58 42 60

History. The House was founded in 1920 and is still
family-owned.

Visiting:	Open daily.
Vineyards:	18 ha – 70% Ch, 20% PN, 10% PM.
Annual Prod:	300,000 bottles.
Exports:	50%.

House Style:	Elegant wines of lightness and great balance.

NV Brut Réserve (60% PN, 40% Ch)
Medium- to full-bodied with a fine, persistent *mousse* and
good *pinot* fruit on the nose with hints of vanilla and
brioche. Good ripe fruit on the palate and a long, clean
finish.

NV Blanc de Blancs Brut (11% Ch)
Attractive and elegant. Good persistent *mousse,* and soft,
ripe fruit on the nose with vanilla, nutty aromas. Mouth-
filling, soft, fresh fruit and a long, lingering finish.

NV Rosé Brut (80% Ch, 20% red PN wine from Bouzy)
A light-bodied, very easy-to-drink *rosé* with great charm.
Soft, fruity, aromatic nose and rich, ripe fruit on the
palate. Good balance and depth, with a long, satisfying
finish.

Vintage Brut 1985 (100% Ch)
Elegant and very drinkable. Very fine, persistent *mousse*
and good, complex *chardonnay* fruit on the nose. Mouth-
filling rounded fruit and a long, clean, crisp finish.

Cuvée Gentilhomme 1982 (100% Ch)
A lovely, elegant, complex wine of great depth and
balance with a really, long lingering finish.

ABEL LEPITRE

Blvd du Val de Vesle, BP 2817, 51055 Reims
Tel: 25 52 65 46

History. The House was created by Abel Lepitre in 1924
in the tiny village of Ludes, at the foot of the Montagne
de Reims. He was born in Champagne and came from a
family which had been growing grapes for generations.

By the end of the 1930s the House was shipping
100,000 bottles a year and developing a reputation both at
home and abroad. Abel died aged 40 and his fourteen-
year-old son Jacques took over. Sales continued to grow
and in 1960 Jacques created Les Grands Champagnes de
Reims. The House is now part of the Marie Brizard group
although still trading under its own name. It also manages
to combine the most modern wine-making techniques,
equipment and marketing with tradition.

Visiting:	The House will be accepting visitors from summer 1992.
Vineyards:	None.
Annual Prod:	300-400,000 bottles.
Exports:	40%.
House Style:	Elegant, delicate wines with good balance and depth.

NV Brut (60% PN, 15% PM, 25% Ch)
A fine, vigorous *mousse*. Floral nose, with lots of ripe fruit on the palate balanced by the freshness and elegance of the *chardonnay*. Well-balanced with a good, long finish.

Vintage Brut (60% PN, 40% Ch)
Matured for a minimum of four years to produce a pale wine with a fine and vigorous *mousse*. It has a delicate, fruity bouquet and is big and rounded in the mouth, with good balance and a firm finish. It is a wine that will improve further with ageing.

NV Cuvée 134 (100% Ch)
Lively, and fresh with a long, lingering finish. Very elegant.

Reserve 'C' Vintage (100% Ch)
A *crémant*, and the speciality of the House. A delicate blend of *cru chardonnay* from a single year. Traditional fermentation gives a soft wine with a gentler *mousse* but still great complexity and depth. Lovely *chardonnay* nose with aromas of apples, dried fruit and vanilla. Well-balanced and elegant. Will age well.

Vintage Rosé Brut (55% PN, 30% Ch, 15% Bouzy red wine from PN)

A pale salmon pink, with a fruity nose full of berry aromas. Big rounded fruit on the palate but fresh and elegant thanks to the *chardonnay*. Good balance.

Cuvée Réservée Abel Lepitré (65% Ch, 35% PN)
A perfumed, flowery nose with good fruit. A big, complex wine of great balance and depth, with a long finish.

MAILLY

29 Rue de la Libération, BP 1,
51500 Mailly Champagne
Tel: 26 49 41 10

History. Founded as a co-operative in 1929 by Gabriel Simon and twenty-three other growers, Mailly is one of the seventeen Houses entitled to label all its bottles *'grand cru'*. The House was established during a period of crisis in Champagne and the intention was to press the members' grapes, and store the wine, until the climate improved and they could get a better price from the champagne Houses. Instead, they decided to produce and market their own wine and they have not looked back since. Today the co-operative has seventy members and the original thirty hectares of vineyards have expanded to seventy hectares. In order to maintain its *grand cru* status all wines produced come from the Mailly vineyards in the Montagne de Reims. The House has more than 1 kilometre of cellars and more than 1.5 million bottles in stock.

Visiting:	Weekdays 9-11 am and 2-5 pm, Saturdays 9-11 am (From 1 to 30 May also open Saturday and Sunday 2-5 pm)

Vineyards:	70 ha (75% PN, 25% Ch).
Annual Prod:	600,000 bottles.
Exports:	50%.
House Style:	Well-structured wines with elegance and maturity.

NV Extra Brut (75% PN, 25% Ch)
A *cuvée* assembled from wines four and five years old with no *dosage*. Golden colour and strong bouquet with vanilla aromas. A big wine, full of flavour but well-balanced and with good length.

NV Brut Réserve (80% PN, 20% Ch)
Produced only from grapes grown in the *grand cru* Mailly Champagne vineyard. A very elegant wine with an intense, distinctive nose and rich, balanced fruit on the palate.

NV Rosé Brut (90% PN, 25% Ch)
The *chardonnay* adds an extra elegance to an already classy wine which spends at least four years on its lees before disgorging. A very attractive, delicate nose and full of *pinot* flavours of redcurrants and berries.

Vintage Brut (75% PN, 25% Ch)
A very attractive nose with vanilla and slightly toasty aromas. Creamy and very vigorous *mousse,* and big and powerful on the palate. A big wine in every sense and will age well.

Cuvée 60ième Anniversaire (60% PN, 40% Ch)
A very delicate but persistent *mousse,* floral nose and big,
rounded fruit flavours in the mouth. *Pinot* backbone
balanced very well by *chardonnay* elegance.

Cuvée des Echansons (75% PN, 25% Ch)
The House showcase wine produced in limited quantities
and only in the most exceptional years. The 1981 and
1982 are currently on offer. A very well-balanced wine
marrying the best of the *pinot* and *chardonnay.* A big
wine with staying power.

MARIE STUART
8 Place de la République, 51059 Reims
Tel: 26 47 92 26

History. The House was founded in 1867 although the name was not registered as a trademark until 1909. The company has had several owners since the 1920s – André Garitant in 1927, Champagne Trouillard in 1954, Prat-Fontaine and Longuet in 1962, and the Société Anonyme Magenta-Epernay (SAME) in 1972. The House moved to its present offices in the 1960s while retaining its original cellars.

Visiting:	None.
Vineyards:	None.
Annual Prod:	1.7 million bottles.
Exports:	35%.

House Style:	Light and fruity.

NV Tradition Brut (60% PN/PM, 40% Ch)
A big, fruity wine on nose and palate, with good balance but a rather abrupt finish.
There is also a *demi-sec.*

NV Brut Rosé (60% PN/PM, 40% Ch)
With 15-20% of red Coteaux Champenois wine, it has a very pale pink colour, with very fine, persistent *mousse.* Fresh and crisp on the palate, with good depth of fruit and a good, lingering finish.

Vintage Brut 1985 (80% Ch, 20% PN)
Medium-bodied with good, persistent *mousse,* and attractive, fruity, floral nose. Good rounded fruit on the palate and well balanced. Sustained finish.

Cuvée R. G. (100% Ch)
A *blanc de blancs* based on *chardonnay* from the Côte des Blancs. An elegant, fruity wine with good acid balance, which makes it very suitable as an aperitif or with fish dishes.

Cuvée de la Reine Marie Stuart (Ch/PN blend)
Mostly *chardonnay* from the Côte des Blancs with *pinot noir* from top vineyards of the Montagne de Reims. An *assemblage* of reserve wines to produce a rich, well-balanced wine with great complexity and depth.

MERCIER

75 Avenue de Champagne, 51200 Epernay
Tel: 26 54 71 11

History. The House was founded in 1858 by Eugène
Mercier who had the idea of creating a champagne empire
able to provide affordable, good wines in large volumes.
To achieve this he established Maison Mercier Union de
Propriétaires, based in Paris. This was an amalgamation
of five established champagne Houses – Berton, Philippe
Bourlon, Dufait Père & Fils, René Lesecq and Veuve
Soyez.

Mercier was, above all, a great showman, and many of
his stunts to promote his champagnes to the population at
large, rather than just to the rich, are legendary. One such
stunt involved building the world's second largest barrel
for the World Exhibition held in Paris in 1889. It was
built in Epernay, weighed 20,000 kilograms empty and
held the equivalent of 215,000 bottles. It required more
than 250 thousand-year-old Hungarian oaks to make it,
and felling the timber, ageing it and construction took

more than twenty years. A team of twenty-four oxen hauled it to Paris and the elaborately-carved barrel was so large that along some parts of the route, houses had to be demolished to allow it to pass. The barrel was returned to Epernay after the exhibition and used for blending until after World War II.

In 1900, Mercier used a giant, tethered, Mercier-emblazoned ballloon to give people a bird's-eye view over the World Exhibition showground, and the same year, at the exhibition, he screened the world's first documentary film. Made by the Lumière brothers in 1898 and commissioned by Mercier, it was called 'From the Grape to the Glass'.

Because of the scale of his operations, small, conventiónal cellars were not suitable, so Mercier set about building a network of wide, straight galleries. There are forty-seven galleries which stretch for more than eighteen kilometres, and five of them are more than 1,200 metres in length.

In the old days, visitors were driven round by horse and carriage. In 1891 the French President Sadi Carnot was driven round the cellars in a coach pulled by four white horses. A car rally was even staged there in the 1950s. Today, Mercier attracts almost 175,000 visitors a year, and they are transported through the cellars on board a miniature electric train.

The cellars hold the equivalent of 15.5 million bottle, and a new visitors' centre has been opened. The House moved to its present address in 1930, and was acquired by Moët & Chandon in 1970. A year later both became part of the giant Moët-Hennessy Group.

Visiting:	Open daily. Electric train and a very enjoyable tour.
Vineyards:	195 ha.
Annual Prod:	5.7 million bottles.
Exports:	29%.
House Style:	A very approachable style with maximum appeal. Elegant wines with intense bouquets and rich, ripe rounded fruit.

NV Brut 1985
Very pale gold in colour with a fine and persistent
mousse. Delicate floral bouquet with hazelnut aromas.
Big and full on the palate, with attractive *meunier* fruit.

NV Rosé Brut (PN/PM Blend)
Intense floral nose with rich, soft berry fruit aromas and
ripe red fruit on the palate, with citrus flavours. Well
balanced with a firm finish.

NV Demi-Sec
Very flowery, honeyed nose with hints of raisins. Big and
rounded on the palate with sweet baked-apple flavours. A
long, clean finish.

Vintage Brut 1986
A complex nose full of floral, vegetable aromas. Very
elegant on the palate with good, fresh *chardonnay* fruit
and grapefruit flavours. Good finish.

Cuvée Bulle d'Or
Mercier's prestige *cuvée* and very elegant, delicate wine
with great balance. Very floral nose with hedgerow flower
aromas. Rich, ripe fruit on the palate which build to an
aromatic, honeyed lingering finish.

MOËT & CHANDON

20 Avenue de Champagne, 51200 Epernay
Tel: 26 54 71 71

History. The House was founded in 1743 and its growth has been phenomenal by any standards – it now accounts for almost a third of all champagne experts.

The Moët family, of Dutch origin, can trace its roots in the champagne region back to the fourteenth century, when Jean and Nicholas Moët were both listed as magistrates in Reims. Certainly, a Moët, in his capacity as magistrate, stood close to Joan of Arc when Charles VII was crowned in Reims Cathedral in 1429.

The House was founded by Claude Moët who owned a number of Marne vineyards. Although it flourished, it was not until 1792, when his grandson Jean-Rémy took control at the age of thirty-four that things started to take off. He developed close links with Napoleon through his position as Mayor of Reims and became supplier to the Court. This quickly led to a brisk export trade with many other European royal courts. Napoleon made a special trip to Moët, shortly before he was exiled to the island of Elba, to present Jean-Rémy with the Légion d'Honneur.

The company has always invested heavily in order to grow, and during the nineteenth century vineyards were acquired and the export market expanded. In 1832 Jean-Remy Moët handed the firm over to his son Victor and his son-in-law Pierre-Gabriel Chandon, and the House took the new name of Moët & Chandon. At the same time the company acquired the abbey at Hautvillers and its vineyards.

It is a tribute to their business skills and extreme optimism that in 1932, when the world was gripped by recession, they chose to launch Dom Pérignon, an unused *marque* they had bought from Mercier two years earlier. Robert-Jean de Vogüé also joined the House in that year and was largely responsible for the company's rapid growth, which continued unabated after World War II. By the 1960s, production was more than 10 million bottles a year and the company's expansion included the acquisition of Ruinart (1963), Mercier (1970), and the Christian Dior perfume house (1971). The House went public in 1962 and was the first Champagne House to be quoted on the Paris Bourse and, after a series of complex deals, it became part of the massive LVMH Group.

Today it retains the largest vineyard holding of any champagne House, with more than 503 hectares of productive vines, although they meet only a fifth of the company's requirements. Everything about Moët is on a massive scale, including the winery, with its massive stainless steel fermentation tanks and even larger blending tanks capable of holding the equivalent of three quarters of a million bottles of champagne. There are more than twenty-nine kilometres of cellars. These and the winery prove a mecca for visitors – more than 150,000 a year.

In 1973 the company acquired 526 hectares in the Napa Valley, California, and in 1974, 121 hectares in Brazil, on which it has built one of South America's most modern wineries. It has since expanded its Californian wine holdings, founded Domaine Chandon in Australia (1985), and the Chandon España vineyard in Spain.

A Moët & Chandon cork pops every second somewhere in the world!

Visiting:	Open daily. Conducted tours, multi-lingual guides.
Vineyards:	503 ha in production. Total holdings (with Mercier) 881 ha of which 748 ha are planted. Mercier has 195 ha in production. The vineyards provide 20% of Moët & Chandon's needs. The vineyards are in the Côte des Blancs – Choilly, Cramant and Le Mesnil; Montagne de Reims – Ambonnay, Bouzy, Mailly-Champagne, Puisieul, Sillery, Verzenay and Verzy; and Vallée de la Marne – Aÿ-Champagne and Tours-sur-Marne.
Annual Prod:	24.5 million bottles, with stocks of 85 million bottles.
Exports:	79%.
House Style:	Wines range from good-value, well-made, firm, fruity wines to outstanding.

NV Brut Imperial (*Première Cuvée* in the UK)
The blend varies each year but is predominantly *pinot noir* usually about half, with about a third *chardonnay* and the remainder *pinot meunier*. Slightly pale yellow in colour with a fine, persistent *mousse*. Delicate, soft bouquet with citrus and *pinot* aromas. Fresh and elegant on the palate, with good ripe *pinot* fuit, and a gentle but full-flavoured finish.

NV Demi-Sec
The blend varies year by year to achieve consistency of style. Generally *pinot noir* and *pinot meunier* in roughly equal measure with about one-fifth *chardonnay*. A rich bouquet full of sweet fruit, raisiny aromas. Big and rounded in the mouth, with a long, sweet finish.

Vintage Brut Impérial 1986 (40% Ch, 30% PN, 30% PM)
Deep gold in colour with a very delicate but vigorous *mousse*. A touch of apricots on the very full, fruity nose, and mouth-filling fruity, nutty, toasty flavours. A big wine with a long finish.

Vintage Brut Imperial Rosé 1986 (50% Ch, 50% PN partly vinified as red wine)
A delicate wine with strong, ripe *pinot* fruit, and rich, fruity, flowery flavours on the palate. Good length and balance.

Cuvée Dom Pérignon 1983 Brut (58% Ch, 42% PN)
Pale gold colour with a very delicate but persistent *mousse*. Very attractive, fragrant, floral nose with aromas of lime. Rich, delicious and complex on the palate with toasty, *brioche,* nutty flavours but light and fragrant with very good balance. A long finisher.

Cuvée Dom Pérignon Rosé 1982 Brut (60% Ch, 40% PN partly vinified as red wine)
A very delicate, peach-pink colour with orange tinges, and a fine, vigorous *mousse*. A rich soft nose with aromas of ripe red fruit and a not unpleasant underlying earthiness. Fresh and elegant on the palate with hints of citrus coming through in the long finish. Delicious.

MONTAUDON

**6 Rue Ponsardin, 51100 Reims
Tel: 26 47 33 30**

History. The House was founded in Epernay in 1891 by
Auguste-Eugène Montaudon who was just nineteen years
old. His father, Auguste-Louis, was employed by a leading
Saumur company in the Loire, and had been sent to
Epernay to learn about champagne. The House moved to
its new premises in erims in 1957, to what was formerly
the home of Champagne van der Gucht, which they had
acquired. The company is still family-owned, under the
control of Luc and Montaudon.

Visiting:	By appointment.
Vineyards:	25 ha of PN.
Annual Prod:	700,000 bottles.
Exports:	20%.
House Style:	Well-balanced wines with good depth.

NV Brut (50% PN, 25% PM, 25% Ch)
Very fine, persistent *mousse,* with a flowery nose. Rich,
rounded fruit on the palate with good balance and depth. A
long, clean, crisp finish.

NV Demi-Sec (50% PN, 25% PM, 25% Ch)
A sweet, flowery nose, and good fruit on the palate
balances the sweetness so that it is not too cloying. A long,
luscious finish.

NV Blanc de Blancs Brut (100% Ch)
Lively and fresh, with a fine, persistent *mousse* and good
chardonnay fruit on nose and palate. Rounded fruit in the
mouth is well balanced by the underlying acidity. A good
finish.

Vintage Brut (50% PN, 50% Ch)
Aged for three to four years, a big wine with very fine,
persistent *mousse,* and complex ripe-fruit and floral nose
with hints of toast, nuts and vanilla. Very good balance on
the palate with a long, satisfying finish.

Vintage Grande Rosé Brut (38% PN, 50% Ch plus 12%
PN red wine from Bouzy)
A medium- to full-bodied, classy *rosé* with firm,
vigorous, creamy *mousse* and rich, red fruit flavours on
the nose and palate. A good finish. A wine that drinks
well with many dishes.

MUMM

G. H. Mumm et Cie, 29 Rue du Champ-de-Mars, 51053 Reims
Tel: 26 49 59 69

History. The House was founded in 1827 as P. A. Mumm & Cie in an elaborate deal between the Mumm brothers from the Rheingau, another German, Friedrich Giesler, and a Reims merchant called Hauser. The Mumms already owned considerable vineyards in Germany and had established a reputation for their wines. Within ten years, Hauser and Giesler had left the company, the latter to set up his own House in Avize. Another Mumm brother, Théophile, was dispatched to Reims to run the company, which he did until his death in 1852. Following his death the company split into two, one part being run by Jules Mumm and the other by Georges-Hermann Mumm. Jules Mumm traded as a company until 1909 before being taken over by G. H. Mumm & Cie, which had seen phenomenal growth. By the turn of the century it had become the largest of the *négociant* houses, and this led, in the 1900s, to a major expansion programme, particularly to increase their vineyard holdings. The company had remarkable success on the American market and exported 1.5 million bottles in 1902.

The Mumms had never sought French naturalisation and because they still held German nationality, their company was confiscated during World War I and its assets auctioned off in 1920. A group of businessmen formed the *Société Vinicole de Champagne Successeur de G. H. Mumm et Cie* to bid, and they were successful. The two principals were Georges Robinet, who had been caretaker General Manager following the company's sequestration, and René Lalou, who was to be the power-house for the next fifty-three years. He had married into the Dubonnet family who were also shareholders. The House expanded, its vineyard acreage doubled and the name of *Cordon Rouge*, launched in 1876, vigorously promoted worldwide.

During World War II, with the Germans in occupation, the original family reclaimed their property and ran it for four years, before it was confiscated again and returned to its French owners, now called G. H Mumm et Cie, Société Vinicole de Champagne – Successeur.

Seagram became shareholders in 1955 and eventually acquired the whole company in 1972. Their investment allowed Mumm's expansion to continue and the winery facilities to be fully modernised. Overseas interests include Domaine Mumm in California.

Visiting:	Weekdays 9-11 am and 2-5 pm.
Vineyards:	213 ha.
Annual Prod:	10.8 million bottles.
Exports:	70%.
House Style:	Wines with personality, great style and elegance, and even greater drinkability. Light, fragrant, fruity wines which tend to be less dry than those of many Houses.

NV Cordon Rouge (45% PN, 25% PM, 20% Ch plus 10% reserve wines)
The House flagship and first produced in 1876 with the basic blend unaltered over the years. Light golden colour with fine but very persistent *mousse*. Soft, fruity nose and rich, creamy, elegance on the palate with ripe fruit. A dry start and a crisp, smooth, lingering finish.

Cordon Rouge Vintage Brut 1985 (70% PN, 30% Ch)
Made from only the best wines in exceptional years. Rich and full-bodied, full of ripe fruit and nutty, toasty flavours, and very well-balanced. Smooth and delicious with a long finish.

Cordon Rosé Vintage Brut 1985 (70% PN, 30% Ch plus red wine from Bouzy)
A very classy *rosé*. Rich, full-bodied with ripe soft fruit and with good depth. The *chardonnay* gives it great elegance and lightness.

Mumm de Cramant Brut (100% Ch)
Once reserved for the Directors of Mumm, the wine is a secret blend of selected wines from Cramant, one of the only two *grand crus* in the Côte des Blancs. Very exclusive. A very fine but persistent *mousse* with elegant *chardonnay* nose with aromas of *brioche* and vanilla. Great lightness and freshness on the palate. Crisp and very elegant.

René Lalou Vintage Brut (50% Ch, 50% PN)
Launched in 1969 and named after the man who directed

the company for more than fifty years. A wine of great elegance and charm. Delicate fruity bouquet, and full of rich fruit flavours on the palate. A wine of great depth and length, with a stunning finish.

Grand Cordon Vintage 1985 (50% Ch, 50% PN)
The 1985 vintage was the first to be released under this new prestige *cuvée* label, launched in 1990 and replacing *Mumm de Mumm*. Only the finest *crus* are selected, with the *pinot noir* coming from the Grande Montagne de Reims and the Vallée de la Marne, and the *chardonnay* from the Côte des Blancs. A big, full-bodied wine with great freshness and liveliness. Very well balanced, with rich fruit, good acidity and an elegant freshness. A big, long finish.

NAPOLÉON

**Ch. & A. Prieur, 2 Rue de Villiers-aux-Bois,
51130 Vertus
Tel: 26 52 11 74**

History. The House was founded in 1825 by Jean-Louis Prieur, who was born in Mailly in 1799 and moved to Vertus at the age of twenty-one. In 1825 he married Marie-Reine Pageot, and established his own champagne House, selling the wines under the Prieur-Pageot label. His sons Charles and Alfred gave their initials to the company. Charles's sons, Louis-Charles and Alfred, who took over the company in 1898, had the brainwave of using the name Napoléon as a *marque*. The family has retained the right ever since to use the names Napoléon and Bonaparte on their wines.

Visiting:	By appointment.
Vineyards:	None.
Annual Prod:	150,000 bottles.
Exports:	60%.

House Style:	Attractive, easy-drinking wines with charm, and vintages that are often outstanding. Good value.

NV Brut (55% PN, 45% Ch)
Easy-drinking wine with sound, vigorous *mousse* and creamy, soft ripe fruit nose. Mouth-filling fruit, but well-balanced and a long, lingering finish.

NV Rosé Brut (55% PN, 45% Ch)
Very elegant wine with fine, sustained *mousse* and attractive soft, ripe red fruit aromas on the nose. Well-rounded, with good *pinot* fruit on the palate and a good, sustained finish.

Vintage Brut (55% PN, 45% Ch)
A big, rich, powerful wine with fine, persistent *mousse,* and elegant, ripe, fruity nose – a foretaste of the great balance between the two grape varieties on the palate. A long, strong finish.

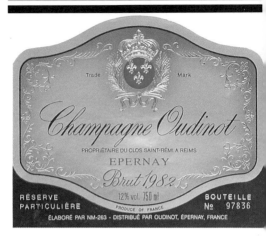

OUDINOT

12 Rue Godart Roger, BP 256, 51207 Epernay
Tel: 26 54 60 31

History. The House was founded at the end of the last
century by Jules Edouard Oudinot, a winegrower in
Avize, who was joined by his son Marcel in the 1940s.
Their *chardonnay* vineyards in the Côte des Blancs
allowed them to produce top-quality wines which quickly
established the reputation of the company. Sales grew
from around 15,000 bottles a year in 1946 to 500,000 by
1979, with a substantial export business.

In 1979 Oudinot took over the House of Jeanmarie in
Châlons-sur-Marne but two years later, because of ill-
health, Marcel sold the company and its vineyards to
Michel Trouillard. The company moved to its present
offices and cellars in 1983 and substantial investments
have been made in new equipment. There are five
kilometres of cellars with a total storage and handling
capacity of 6 million bottles.

Visiting:	By appointment only.
Vineyards:	80 ha; Avize 10 ha, Cramant 8 ha and
	Choilly 12 ha – all *chardonnay;*
	Tauxiéres 8 ha, Les Mesneux 3 ha,
	Villedommange 3 ha, Orbais l'Abbaye

	7.5 ha, Reims 4.5 ha, Dizy 5 ha, Champillon 7 ha, others 12 ha – all *pinot noir*.
Annual Prod:	1.5 million bottles.
Exports:	50-55%.
House Style:	Wines of great finesse.

NV Brut (40% PN, 30% PM, 30% Ch)
A blend of thirty different wines and reserve wines.
Golden yellow colour with fine, persistent *mousse*. An
elegant and fruity nose, fresh and fruity on the palate with
good balance and long finish.

NV Blanc de Blancs (100% Ch)
Yellow with green tints, and a strong but fine *mousse*. A
rich bouquet of berries and ripe fruit, and good fresh fruit
on the palate. Long finish.

NV Rosé Brut (70% PN, 30% PM)
Quite a dark pink with fine, persistent *mousse*. A rich
bouquet of berries and ripe fruit, and good fresh fruit on
the palate. Long finish.

Cuvée Particulière Rosé 1982 (100% PN)
Aged for seven years to produce a brilliant onion-skin
colour. Fine, vigorous *mousse,* warm, delicate berry
bouquet and soft, ripe fruit on the palate.

Vintage Blanc de Blancs Brut 1982 (100% Ch)
A blend of the best wines from three *grand cru* vineyards
owned by Oudinot – Avize, Cramant and Chouilly. Aged
for more than seven years to produce a golden yellow
wine with fine, persistent *mousse* and great elegance.
Complex, toasty, floral nose, but full of freshness, fruit
and complexity on the palate, with a long, lingering finish.

ÉLABORÉ PAR NM-263-DISTRIBUÉ PAR OUDINOT, EPERNAY, FRANCE

Vintage Brut 1985 (55% PN, 35% Ch, 10% PM)
A blend of twenty different *cuvées* from the Montagne de
Reims and Côte de Blancs, all 100% *grand cru.* Yellow-
gold with fine, persistent *mousse,* and an attractive,
complex nose bursting with flowery, fruity aromas. Very
fresh in the mouth with good ripe fruit, good balance and a
long, steady finish.

Vintage Rosé Brut 1985 (100% PN)
A blend of several *pinot noir grand cru cuvées,* vinified
as *rosé* and aged for a minimum of four years. A brilliant
onion-skin colour with fine, persistent *mousse.* Elegant on
the palate with good, soft, curranty, berry fruit. Long,
gentle finish.

Vintage Cuvée Blanc de Noirs 1985 (85% PN, 15% PM)
A blend of wines from ten different vineyards in the
Montagne de Reims, 100% *grand cru.* Brilliant golden
yellow colour with a strong but fine *mousse.* Big, fruity,
aromatic nose, and bursting with fruit in the mouth. Well-
balanced and classy.

BRUNO PAILLARD

**Avenue de Champagne, 51100 Reims
Tel: 26 36 20 22**

History. The House was founded in 1981 and was awarded *négociant-manipulant* status by the CICC three years later. Although the youngest House in Champagne, it has already acquired a remarkable reputation for the quality of its wines. Bruno comes from a long line of *vignerons* and brokers, and his father Rémy has already developed a flourishing BOB champagne business on the home market. Bruno, born in 1953, joined the family firm in 1975 as a broker but was also acting as a consultant to the largest BOB champagne firm, Marne & Champagne, and trading as a BOB broker. As a result, he was often abe to buy the best wines available and rather than sell them on for BOB, he decided to establish his own *marque* and sell the wine himself. He initially started trading as a *marque d'achetuer* and acquired full NM status in 1984.

The wines are made and stored in an ultra-modern air-conditioned facility built on the Epernay road on the outskirts of Reims. The House specialises in the production of NV luxury *cuvées* and vintages. The wine is produced by the traditional method, from the best possible grapes in the Champagne area, under the personal supervision of the owner.

Visiting:	By appointment.
Vineyards:	None.
Annual Prod:	350,000 bottles.
Exports:	95%.
House Style:	Elegance above all, but wines of freshness, youth and flavour. The *dosage* is kept as low as possible and every bottle carries the date of its *dégorgement*.

NV Première Cuvée Brut (45% PN, 33% Ch, 22% PM)
The wine is produced exclusively from the first pressing, hence its name. Grapes from about thirty different villages are selected and the wines are then blended with reserve wines, the proportions of which are kept a closely-guarded secret. This wine represents sixty per

cent of the House's sales, and is their flagship wine. A wine of balance and great complexity, with a wonderful nose of flowery, ripe fruit, and citrus aromas. Very dry in the mouth with notable acidity but perfectly balanced by the fruit. A long, long finish.

NV Première Cuvée Rosé Brut (85% PN, 15% Ch)
Again produced exclusively from the first pressing. A true *brut* with low *dosage* and delicate red fruit aromas. A very delicate, underripe strawberry-pink colour with fine, frothy, vigorous *mousse*. Very delicate and fragrant on the palate with soft fruit.

Chardonnay Réserve Privée (100% Ch)
Produced from grapes from only the Côte des Blancs and the Côte de Sézanne. Pale straw in colour with a very delicate but persistent *mousse*. A rich bouquet full of toasty, fruity aromas and hints of citrus, vanilla and sweetness, but very dry on the palate.

Vintage Brut 1985 (20% PN, 80% Ch)
Still remarkably fresh with rich *pinot* fruit, but having great depth and complexity. Very vigorous, fine *mousse* with rich, fruity, almost honeyed nose. A big, very classy, mouth-filling wine with a very long, lingering finish. The label was illustrated by Jean-Yves Gosti, a young French artist living in Paris.

Vintage Brut Blanc de Blancs 1983 (100% Ch)
A delicate wine with elegant floral nose and very dry on the palate. Great balance and harmony, with good soft fruit and a long finish. The label was created by French painter Bernard Piffaretti who was asked to illustrate the theme 'balance'.

Vintage Brut 1979 (90% Ch, 10% PN)
Elegant and mature but retaining great freshness because of the late disgorging. Brilliant, clear golden colour with tints of green, and a delicate bouquet with aromas of almonds and vanilla. Elegant with lively fruit on the palate and a long satisfying finish.

Other recommended vintages: 1976, 1975 and 1969.

PALMER

57 Rue Jacquart, 51100 Reims
Tel: 26 07 35 07

History. This co-operative was founded by seven prominent champagne growers at Avize in 1947, and the Palmer brand was created the following year. The members were all owners of vineyards in the *grand cru* districts of Avize, Bouzy, Ludes, Rilly and Verzenay. They use only their own grapes, harvested from twenty-seven different *crus* – half *chardonnay* and half red – *pinot noir* and *pinot meunier*.

The House relocated to larger premises in Reims in 1959 and has continued to expand ever since. The cellars now cover one hectare. The House is owned by the *Société de Producteurs des Grands Terroirs de Champagne* and now has 150 members. It is claimed the House derives its name from Huntley & Palmer biscuits – very fashionable in post-war France – because the founding members could not agree among themselves upon any other title. Whatever the origin of the name, Palmer is one of the outstanding co-operative producers which is deservedly gaining international recognition.

Visiting:	By appointment.
Vineyards:	300 ha.
Annual Prod:	300,000 bottles carry the Champagne

	Palmer label. Total annual production of the Société is 1.5 million bottles.
Exports:	35%.
House Style:	Good value, good quality, easy-drinking wines with style and maturity.

NV Brut (50% Ch, 40% PN, 10% PM)
Very fine, persistent *mousse* and elegant nose full of fruity aromas. Good ripe fruit on the palate with apple flavours, and a strong, clean, crisp finish. Good value.

NV Rosé Brut Rubis (50% Ch, 50% PN/PM with red wine added)
Soft, creamy, raspberry-fruity on the nose and good ripe fruit on the palate. Well-balanced with some depth and a good finish.

Vintage Brut (40% PN, 10% PM, 50% Ch)
Big, complex nose full of floral and appley aromas. Full-bodied with ripe fruit on the palate. A biscuity, toasty, crisp finish.

Vintage Blanc de Blancs Brut (100% Ch)
Delicate and light, with soft, creamy-fruity nose and vanilla aromas. Full and rounded on the palate with a long, clean, lingering finish.

Cuvée Amazone (50% Ch, 50% PN)
A wine of elegance and depth. Fuller-bodied than the vintage with greater depth and richness because of much higher levels of reserve wines – up to a fifth. Good value.

PANNIER

Société Coopérative Vinicole de la Vallée de la Marne (SCVM Pannier), 23 Rue Roger Catillon, 02400 Château-Thierry
Tel: 23 69 13 10

History. In 1889 Louis-Eugène Pannier founded his wine business at Château-Thierry. In 1929 his son Gaston started to produce Pannier Champagne at Dizy, close to Épernay, and it became so successful that it quickly outgrew its cellars.

This problem was resoved in 1937 when Pannier acquired a thirteenth-century stone quarry at Château-Thierry. It had been hollowed out on two levels thirty metres below the ground, and provided the space and ideal conditions required for storing and ageing the wines. The cellars can hold 8 million bottles.

Gaston died in 1955 leaving a thriving business, and in 1971 a group of vine growers acquired the House. Basing its strategy on strict quality control and permanent reinvestment, Pannier continues to prosper. Betwen 1971 and 1989 shipments rose from 160,000 bottles to 2.2 million bottles, and exports increased dramatically.

Visiting: Open daily. Ring 23 69 13 10 for conducted tours.

Vineyards:	400 ha in the Vallée de la Marne, Montagne de Reims and Côte des Blancs. Only grapes from its 200 members are used.
Annual Prod:	3 million bottles.
Exports:	20%.
House Style:	Rounded, elegant wines with strong *pinot meunier* influence.

NV Tradition Carte Noire Brut (predominantly PM with a little Ch)
A very elegant wine. Attractive nose with toasty, hazelnut aromas. Young, fresh and very well-balanced, with a good finish.

NV Rosé (predominantly PM)
A reddish-pink *rosé* with a discreet nose and soft fruit on the palate. Not an assertive wine.

Vintage Brut 1985 (85% PM, 20% PN, 34% Ch)
Elegant, floral nose, mouth-filling ripe fruit and good balance with a long, firm finish.

Egérie de Pannier 1985 (46% PM, 20% PN, 34% Ch)
A very elegant wine, pale gold in colour with a firm, vigorous *mousse,* a soft delicate nose but full fruit on the palate. Well-balanced and with a steady finish.

Maison fondée en 1825

Joseph Perrier fils & Cie

Châlons-sur-Marne

CHAMPAGNE
Cuvée Royale   PRODUCE OF FRANCE

As supplied to
Their Late Majesties
QUEEN VICTORIA
& KING EDWARD VII

750ml   NM-266-001
ÉLABORÉ PAR JOSEPH PERRIER - CHÂLONS-sur-MARNE - FRANCE   ALC. 12% BY VOL.

JOSEPH PERRIER

**59 Avenue de Paris, BP 31, 51015 Châlons-sur-Marne
Tel: 26 58 29 51**

History. The company was founded at the end of the
eighteenth century by Alexandre Perrier, under the name
Perrier & Fils. The House and the brand, however, were
effectively created by his son Joseph in 1825 when he
took control of the company. For the next thirty-five years
he developed the House and its reputation. On his death in
1870 the founder's grandson Gabriel became head of the
firm. He relinquished it in 1888, because he had no heir, to
Paul Pithois, head of a respected and very old wine
company.

The House still belongs entirely to the family with Jean-
Claude Fourmon as chairman. The House maintains its
press house at Cumières, close to its most important
vineyards, and the new wine is then taken to Châlons for
storage. There are three kilometres of chalk cellars,
transformed at the end of the last century from a Roman
quarry. The House belongs to the *Syndicat de Grandes
Marques.*

Visiting:	By appointment. Monday to Thursday, 9-11 am and 2-4 pm. Friday 9-11 am. Closed August.
Vineyards:	20 ha in the Vallée de la Marne, mainly in Hautvillers, Cumières and Damery.

Annual Prod:	750,000 bottles.
Exports:	50-55%.
House Style:	Very well-made, attractive, easy-drinking, elegant, fruity wines.

Maison fondée en 1825

Joseph Perrier fils & Cie
Châlons-sur-Marne

CHAMPAGNE
Cuvée Royale   PRODUCE OF FRANCE
750ml

As supplied to
Their Late Majesties
QUEEN VICTORIA
& KING EDWARD VII

ALC. 12% BY VOL.

ELABORÉ PAR JOSEPH PERRIER - CHALONS-sur-MARNE - FRANCE

NV Cuvée Royale Brut (33.3% PN, 33.3% PM, 33.3% Ch)
Fine, vigorous *mousse,* fresh, ripe fruit and hazelnut nose, and well-structured on the palate. Each of the grapes contributes harmoniously to its elegance and depth.

NV Cuvée Royale Blanc de Blancs (100% Ch)
Lovely, soft, delicate, floral and aromatic on both nose
and palate. Creamy, fruity elegance.

NV Cuvée Royale Rosé Brut (70% PM/PN, 30% Ch)
Dark pink in colour with a fine, persistent *mousse,* and
big *pinot* nose. Well-balanced with traces of sweetness
and a long finish.

Vintage Cuvée Royale Brut 1985 (50% Ch, 50% PN/PM)
A big wine in every sense, with powerful ripe fruit
aromas, mouth-filling rich fruit, and a long strong finish.
Still very youthful, but elegant and will get even better
with further ageing.

Other recommended vintages, 1982 and 1979. All the
declared vintages have great longevity.

There is also a *NV Cuvée Royale Demi-Sec.*

PERRIER-JOUËT

25 Avenue de Champagne, 51200 Epernay
Tel: 26 55 20 53

History. The House was founded in 1811 by Pierre
Nicolas Marie Perrier, who was born in Epernay and was
uncle to Joseph Perrier. In order to avoid confusion, as
there were a number of other Perrier Houses around at the
time, he added the name of his wife, Adèle Jouët, to the
company. It became Perrier-Jouët, now affectionately
known as PJ throughout the wine trade. It has extensive
vineyard holdings and owns one of the loveliest vineyards
in all Champagne.

The company has been in its present premises since
1813 and sent its first shipments of champagne to Britain
in 1815, and to the United States in 1837. The founder's
son Charles expanded the company and substantially
increased exports, particularly to Britain. The wine was
one of the favourites of Queen Victoria and the favourite
of Edward VII. It was also popular with Napoléon III and
King Leopold of the Belgians.

Charles was a prominent Mayor of Reims and a great
ambassador for Champagne, and by the time of his death,
PJ production topped one million bottles a year. He built
Château Perrier, a magnificent baroque mansion, in the
Avenue de Champagne, opposite the company's offices,
and today it houses the town library and museum. Charles
had no heir and left the company to his nephew Henri
Gallice. Then in 1934 it passed to Louis Budin who had
married into the family. In 1959 Michael Budin took over
and although the company was then acquired by Seagram
it still retains remarkable independence.

The Belle Epoque bottle, for which PJ is also famous,
was created by Emile Gallé, who was then commissioned
by Henri Gallice to design a collection. For whatever
reason, the wines were not sold in the Gallé bottles for
very long, and it was not until 1964 that a number of the
originals were re-discovered. The bottle was recreated
and launched in Paris in 1966 to celebrate the seventieth
birthday of Duke Ellington. Today it is used for their
Prestige Cuvée Belle Epoque Fleur de Champagne,
which is regarded internationally as one of the very great
champagnes.

Visiting:	By appointment.
Vineyards:	108 ha including 39 ha Côte des Blancs in Cramant, Avize and Crus.
Annual Prod:	3.2 million bottles.
Exports:	70%.

House Style:	Light delicate wines with great fragrance and depth.

NV Grand Brut (40% PN, 30% PM, 30% Ch)
Very vigorous, persistent *mousse,* and fresh, floral, grassy nose with creamy, yeasty undertones. Very fresh, fruity and youthful on the palate with good acidity and a gentle finish.

NV Blason de France Brut (60% PN/PM, 40% Ch)
Very delicate wine with a fine but very vigorous *mousse.* Soft, creamy nose with attractive yeasty aromas and great balane of rich fruit, youthful elegance and acidity. A big finisher.

NV Blason de France Brut Rosé (60% PN/PM, 20% Ch plus red wine from Bouzy)
A *cuvée spéciale,* and a very delicate rose colour with orange tints. Creamy and flowery on the nose with aromas of *brioche* and red fruits. Big rich *pinot* fruit on the palate which tails off to a gentle but satisfying finish.

Vintage Réserve Cuvée Brut 1985 (40% PN, 30% PM, 30% Ch)
Very typical of the House style with very attractive soft, creamy, yeasty, toasty aromas and rich, ripe fruit on the palate. A wine of great depth, balance and complexity with a long finish.

Belle Epoque Brut 1983 (50% Ch, 50% PN)
A wine of grace and elegance with a rich, golden colour and fine but persistent *mousse.* Very attractive nose full of *brioche* and vanilla aromas, and great balance and depth on the palate with a good finish.

Belle Epoque Brut Rosé 1985 (50% Ch, 50% PN with red wine from Bouzy)
A pale, salmony pink with delicate but persistent *mousse* and wonderful, fresh, floral, almost perfumed nose. Medium-bodied but soft, full of fruit flavours and a touch of attractive grassiness. Finishes well.

PHILIPPONNAT

13 Rue du Pont, Mareuil-sur-Aÿ, 51160 Aÿ
Tel: 50 60 43

History. The House ws founded in 1910 by Pierre
Philipponat, but the family can trace its roots back 500
yers in the Vallée de la Marne. On July 28, 1697 Pierre
Philipponnat registered the coat of arms which is now the
symbol of the firm. The family started to grow its own
grapes at Mareuil-sur-Aÿ around the middle of the
seventeenth century but did not start to sell their own
wines until 1910, when Pierre and Auguste Philipponnat
set up the company.

In 1912 the House moved to Mareuil, and in 1935
acquired the highly acclaimed 5.5 ha Clos des Goisses
vineyard, which produces excellent single vintage, single
estate wines. The House was bought by Gosset in 1980
and acquired by Marie Brizard in 1987.

Since then the House has begun an expansion
programme to increase growth while preserving its
reputation for quality. The House's vineyards provide
about a quarter of its needs and their wines are stored in
two kilometres of chalk cellars, thirty metres below
ground.

Visiting:	By appointment.
Vineyards:	11 ha in the Vallée de la Marne including the 5.5 ha Clos des Goisses (PN/Ch). The other vineyards are around Mareuil-sur-Aÿ (Ch/PN, and Avenay and Murigny (PN).
Annual Prod:	600,000 bottles.
Exports:	62%.
House Style:	Soft, easy-drinking wines of elegance and charm, usually with quite high proportions of reserve wines.

Royale Réserve Brut NV (70% PN/PM, 30% Ch)
A fresh and fruity wine with firm, vigorous *mousse* and
attractive nose. Soft ripe fruit on the palate and a long
finish.

Royale Réserve Brut Rosé NV (70% PN/PM, 30% Ch)
A delicate pink with fine, persistent *mousse* and soft,
creamy fruity bouquet. Soft, rich fruity on the palate,
good balance and a firm finish.

Réserve Speciale Brut Vintage 1985 (70% PN/PM, 30%
Ch)
A big, vigorous champagne with a rich, complex bouquet
and firm, ripe fruit on the palate. Good balance and a very
long finish.

Cuvée Première Grand Blanc 1985 Brut (100% Ch)
A *blanc de blancs,* very dry, elegant and attractive. Fine
but persistent *mousse,* fresh flowery nose and good rich
fruit which gradually asserts itself in the mouth. A
satisfying finish.

Clos des Goisses (70% PN, 30% Ch)
The produce of a single vineyard, and vinified and
matured in oak casks to produce a powerful wine of great
character and complexity. Aged for at least six years, it
has a strong, vigorous *mousse* but fresh, youthful nose
full of fragrant, floral aromas. On the palate it has much
more depth with big, rich fruit and a host of other flavours
– toast and nuts, vanilla and honey. A very long finish and
a wine which will improve further and develop more
complexity with age.

JULES PIERLOT

15 Rue Henri-Martin, 51205 Epernay
Tel: 26 54 45 52

History. A small House founded in 1889 which concentrates on making lightish, high-quality wines.

Visiting:	By appointment.
Vineyards:	None.
Annual Prod:	150,000 bottles.
Exports:	30%.

House Style:	Attractive, light, easy-drinking wines.

NV Carte Rouge Brut (100% PN/PM)
Easy-drinking, attractive style with good, vigorous *mousse* and rich, ripe red fruit on the nose and palate. Long, clean and crisp finish.

NV Casque d'Or Brut (100% PN/PM)
A well-balanced wine with good depth of fruit on nose and palate, and a long, firm finish.

Cuvée Speciale Brut (100% Ch)
Elegant and appealing. Fine, persistent *mousse* and soft, rich fruit on nose and palate. Good depth and balance and a long, lingering finish.

Carte Blanche Blanc de Blancs Brut (100% Ch)
A very attractive, lively wine with fine, persistent *mousse,* and good fresh fruity aromas with hints of *brioche* and vanilla. Good, rounded fruit on the palate and lively acidity. Long, clean finish.

PIPER-HEIDSIECK

51 Blvd Henri-Vasnier, 51100 Reims
Tel: 26 85 01 94

History. The House was founded in 1834 by Christian
Heidsieck. He was one of the three nephews drafted in by
Florenz-Louis Heidsieck to help him run the House he had
founded in 1795. The nephews were Charles-Henri, who
died in 1824, Henri-Louis Walbaum and Christian
Heidsieck. Florenz-Louis died in 1828 and Henri-Louis
and Christian, who could not get on, went their separate
ways in 1834. Christian Heidsieck continued to use the
Heidsieck *marque* and when he died a year later, his
widow ran the company as Veuve Heidsieck. In 1837 she
married Henri Piper, her brother-in-law, and the House
changed its name yet again, this time to H. Piper & Cie,
although still using the Heidsieck *marque.*

In 1845 the company became Piper Heidsieck and that
year Charles-Camille, son of Charles-Henri, joined the
firm. In 1850 Jean-Claude Kunkelmann, who had been the
House's American agent, returned to Reims and became a
partner in the company, and a year later Charles-Camille
left to join Henriot before establishing his own House. In
1870, when Henri Piper died, Kunkelmann took over the
company and changed its name to his own. Kunkelmann
& Cie passed to his son Ferdinand in 1881, then to his
daughter, the Marquise Saurez d'Aulan, in 1930.

Her son François now runs the company, which was
taken over by Rémy Martin in 1988. The House has ultra-
modern facilities and has been responsible for many wine-
making innovations.

Visiting:	Open weekdays all year, weekends April-November. Electric train.
Vineyards:	None.
Annual Prod:	5.5 million bottles.
Exports:	55%.
House Style:	The wines do not undergo malolactic fermentation and therefore require greater ageing to soften initial austerity. They are mature wines with great depth and flavour which improve further with ageing.

NV Cuvée Brut (55% PN, 30% PM, 15% Ch)
A brilliant, pale, straw-coloured wine with a lively, persistent *mousse*. It is fruity and lively on the nose with aromas of spring flowers and hints of toastiness and honey. On the palate fresh fruity flavours dominate with touches of grapefruit and apple giving a light, crisp, freshness which rounds off in the mouth to a long, fruity finish.

NV Rosé Brut (45% PN, 40% PM, 15% Ch)
A lively wine with bright pink colour and fine, vigorous *mousse*. It is soft but with rich, ripe fruit on the palate. Good as an aperitif or with a wide range of dishes.

Vintage Brut 1985 (55% PN, 15% PM, 30% Ch)
A fine, persistent *mousse* and mature nose with ripe fruit, toasty and nutty aromas. Elegant, mouth-filling rich fruit with good depth and a long, lush finish.

Sauvage 1982 (70% PN, 30% Ch)
A lovely golden colour with green tints, and a very fine but vigorous *mousse*. Very elegant, floral bouquet but needs time for the full rich fruit flavours to develop in the mouth. A long, lingering, almost honeyed finish.

Rare 85 (35% PN, 65% Ch)
The House's *Cuvée de Prestige* launched to commemorate the 200th anniversary of the founding of the original Heidsieck House by Florenz-Louis in 1785. Only produced in exceptional years. A brilliant golden colour with greenish tints and a vigorous, fine *mousse*. On the nose it is aromatic and creamy with hints of vanilla, and soft, damp leather. The nose will develop great complexity as it ages. In the mouth it is bursting with yeasty, vanilla flavours which give way to ripe fruit and a touch of citrus, the special Piper-Heidsieck touch.

PLOYEZ-JACQUEMART

8 Rue Astoin, 51500 Ludes
Tel: 26 61 11 87

History. Found in 1930 and now in its third generation, this small family-owned champagne House is dedicated to preserving the traditional methods necessary to create extraordinary champagne.

The House can trace its origins back to 1868 when Francine Cousinet bought a vineyard in Ludes in the Montagne de Reims. One of her daughters, Noëlly, married Charles Jacquemart and in 1930 their daughter Yvonne, and her husband Marcel Ployez, acquired the vineyard. They decided to make their own wine, rather than simply sell the grapes as the family had been doing for the previous sixty years or so. Yvonne survived her husband and when she died in 1967, the House passed to her two sons Jacques and Gérard. In 1975 Jacques sold his share to Gérard, who had to sell off most of his vineyards to finance the deal.

Today, annual production is less than 6,700 cases and the grapes selected for this come from their remaining plots of 35-year-old *pinot* vines adjoining the *chais* at Ludes, and their small *grand cru* Mailly-Champagne vineyards. The rest, almost all of top *échelle,* is specially selected by Gérard Ployez, mainly from Mesnil-sur-Oger, Cuis, Cramant, Bisseuil, Tauxière and Villers-Marmery. From this he and his daughter Laurence, create a final *assemblage* of roughly equal parts *pinot* and *chardonnay.* The grapes are pressed using the traditional slow process, and the bottle fermentation takes place in the deepest part of the cellar, more than twenty-three metres below ground. This slow and careful ageing process is largely responsible for the very fine *mousse* for which the House is noted.

Visiting:	Open daily. Tasting facilities and restaurant.
Vineyards:	Almost 2 ha.
Annual Prod:	90,000 bottles.
Exports:	70-75%.
House Style:	Elegant, soft, creamy wines with good fruit and balance. Very good value.

NV Brut (50% Ch, 50% PN/PM)
Very fine but persistent *mousse,* and rich creamy nose,
full of soft fruit and *brioche* aromas. Rich, rounded fruit
on the palate with very good balance of acidity, and a
long, powerful finish.

NV Grand Réserve Rosé (50% Ch, 42.5% PN, 7.5% PM)
Peachy-pink in colour with very fine, persistent *mousse.*
Creamy and soft fruit on the nose, and clean, mouth-
filling fruit on the palate. Very drinkable. Good finish.

Vintage Grand Réserve 1985 (50% Ch, 42.5% PN, 7.5%
PM)
A very elegant wine, soft and creamy, with attractive
complex nose. Rich, mature fruit on the palate, and a big
finisher. A wine that will benefit from keeping.

Vintage Grand Réserve Blanc de Blancs 1985 (100% Ch)
Marvellous nose with soft fruit and developing toasty
aromas. Still young on the palate but good fruit with
depth and length. A wine that will drink even better in a
few years.

Cuvée Liesse d'Harbonville 1982 (50% Ch, 50% PN)
A presige *cuvée* of quality. The wine has a very fine but
steady *mousse* of tiny bubbles. The nose is soft and
creamy, with fruity, floral, hazelnut aromas and a hint of
toastiness. It blossoms on the palate with its mouth-filling
fruit but has great balance and a long, lingering finish.

The 1985 vintage is the first to be fermented in barrels.
There is no malolactic fermentation, so the wine will need
to be held longer before bottling.

POL ROGER

1 Rue Henri Lelarge, 51206 Epernay
Tel: 26 55 41 95

History. The House of Roger was founded in 1849 by
eighteen-year-old Pol Roger, It quickly developed a
reputation and in 1876 the first exports were shipped to
Britain. On Pol's death in 1899 his two sons Maurice and
Georges took over the firm and a year later they renamed
the House Pol Roger.

Maurice was Mayor of Epernay when the Germans
occupied the town in 1914 and his heroism during this
period has become legendary. When he finally refused to
stand for office in 1935 he became the first person ever to
be appointed honorary mayor for life.

Pol Roger has always been a popular champagne in
England and the link was further cemented by Sir
Winston Churchill. He preferred it to all the other Houses,
and became one of champagne's greatest ambassadors.

When Maurice died, his son Jacques and nephew Guy
took control, and they were followed by the founder's
two great-grandsons, both named Christian.

Visiting:	By appointment.
Vineyards:	91 ha.
Annual Prod:	1.45 million bottles.
Exports:	65%. Britain and the United States are the two major export markets.
House Style:	Wines of great freshness, style and verve, with remarkable longevity.

NV White Foil Brut/Dry (33% Ch, 33% PN, 33% PM)
Fresh and fruity. Good floral aromas and ripe *pinot
meunier* fruit on the nose, and rich, rounded fruit on the
palate. A wine of great balance and depth with a long,
off-dry finish.

NV Sec (33% Ch, 33% PN, 33% PM)
A fine, persistent *mousse* with a soft, warm, fruity nose.
Good rounded fruit on the palate with balancing acidity,
so not overly sweet. Long, lingering finish.

Vintage 1985 Extra Dry (60% PN, 40% Ch)
An attactive, brilliant golden colour with green tints and a

fine, sustained *mousse*. Lovely soft, flowery nose with *brioche* aromas and big and firm on the palate with rounded, ripe fruit. Very well balanced with depth and a long finish.

Blanc de Chardonnay 1985 Brut (100% Ch)
Very elegant with fine, persistent *mousse* and soft, rich nose full of fruity, floral and vanilla aromas. Rich soft fruit on the palate which develops in intensity to give a very long, satisfying finish.

Vintage Rosé 1985 (60% PN, 40% Ch, plus 15% red wine from Bouzy)
Light in colour but with a massive bouquet that is elegant, attractive, floral, aromatic and packed with ripe *pinot* fruit. Even more powerful on the palate, with mouth-filling flavours of creamy, ripe berry fruit. Long, clean finish.

Cuvée Sir Winston Churchill 1982 (a Ch/PN blend but proportions undisclosed)
I remember the launch of this special *cuvée* at Blenheim Palace in 1984 as it was the first time I had been in a marquee with crystal chandeliers! A big wine with a big price tag, but worth it. Very elegant and approachable. Fine, persistent *mousse*, and soft, flowery, fruity nose. Round, ripe fruit on the palate and very drinkable.

Cuvée Spéciale PR 1982 (50% PN, 50% Ch)
Very fine but vigorous *mousse,* and full of soft, ripe *pinot* fruit on the nose. A very elegant wine, rich and creamy on the palate with superb balance and great depth. A lovely finish.

POMMERY

5 Place du Général Gouraud, 51000 Reims
Tel: 26 05 05 01

History. The House was founded in 1836 by Narcisse Greno, and twenty years later Louis Pommery joined the company. When he died in 1858, his widow Louise Pommery, another of the legendary champagne widows, took over. It is now part of the BSN Group which also owns Lanson. Its full name is Pommery & Greno.

One of Mme Pommery's finest acquisitions was an area of Roman chalk pits ou;ide Reims – the Butte Saint Nicaise – on which she built a series of magnificent buildings, all said to be based on English and Scottish stately homes. She used the eighteen kilometres of Roman-excavated cellars below to store the wines. The family bought many parcels of land and one was used by Pommery's son-in-law, the Comte de Polignac, to build the Château de Crayères – now a hotel. Another was bequeathed to the people of Reims as a park and sporting centre, and is now known as the Parc Pommery.

Visiting:	Open daily throughout the year.
Vineyards:	300 ha – *chardonnay* and *pinot noir.*
Annual Prod:	5.7 million bottles.
Exports:	75%.
House Style:	Well-made wines bursting with flavour, and having great depth and length. Always good value.

NV Brut Royal (30% PN, 30% Ch, 40% PM)
Generous proportions of reserve wines make this a well-above-average NV wine. Very attractive nose with floral, fruity aromas and a fine, persistent *mousse.* Big, fresh, ripe fruit on the palate with very good balance and depth. A long, satisfying finish. There is also a *Sec* and a *Demi-Sec* produced from the same blend.

NV Rosé Brut (34% Ch, 66% PN)
A very good *rosé* using only the best *crus.* A very fine, delicate but persistent *mousse* with a very attractive, delicate nose with hints of freshly cut hay, nuts and toast. Surprisingly big and rounded on the palate with rich, ripe

fruit and good balance and depth. A long, satisfying finish.

Vintage Brut (50% PN, 50% Ch)
An elegant wine with remarkable freshness and fruit. Great balance and depth and a very long finish. Will continue to improve further with ageing.

Vintage Blanc de Blancs (100% Ch)
Elegant and medium-bodied with a very fine, persistent *mousse,* and soft, creamy, ripe fruit nose. Full of fruit on the palate with very good depth and balance. Long, lingering, clean finish.

Louise Pommery (60% Ch, 40% PN)
Chardonnay from Avize and Cramant, and *pinot noir* from Aÿ produce this excellent prestige *cuvée,* which is full-bodied, rich and delicious. *Chardonnay* elegance shines through but the *pinot* fruit gives depth and body. Very well balanced with a long, clean, crisp finish.

RENAUDIN

**Domaines des Conardins, 51200 Moussey-Epernay
Tel: 25 54 03 41**

History. The House was founded in 1935, although the
Domaines des Conardins has a long vine-growing
tradition dating back several centuries. A magnificent
Château on the estate was the home of the noble de Failly
family but it was demolished in 1799 after being wrecked
by prisoners-of-war held there.

The House is now run by Thérèse Renaudin, who
succeeded her father Raymond, and she is assisted by her
two sons Christophe and Dominique Tellier. The
Domaine has twenty-three hectares of champagne
appellation vineyards located around Epernay and the
Côte des Blancs.

Visiting:	By appointment.
Vineyards:	24 ha, 74% PM, 24% Ch, 2% PN.
Annual Prod:	300,000 bottles.
Exports:	55-60%.

House Style:	Well-made floral wines with full rounded fruit and long, lingering finish.

NV Brut Grand Reservé (40% Ch, 60% PN/PM)
A medium- to full-bodied wine with very fine, persistent
mousse, and attractive floral, ripe fruit nose with hints of
hot, fresh bread and new-mown hay. Big, rounded fruit
on the palate with good balance and depth but finishes
abruptly.

NV Brut Rosé (80% PN/PM, 20% Ch)
A little red wine from Moussy is added to achieve the
light delicate pink colour. Fine, persistent *mousse,* and
good soft, ripe red fruit aromas on the nose. Good clean
finish.

Vintage Brut Grand Réserve (PN/Ch blend does not
apply)
A yellow-golden colour with fine but vigorous *mousse.*
Complex, floral, nutty nose with *brioche* and vanilla
aromas, and good ripe fruit on the palate. Lingering
finish.

Cuvée Brut Réserve C. D. (80% Ch, 20% PN/PM)

Produced only in exceptional years, a wine of great finesse and delicacy with very good balance and depth, and a long, clean, crisp finish.

Cuvée Comte Renaud de Failly 1985 (70% Ch, 30% PN/PM)
Dedicated to Pierre-Louis, Comte de Failly, who was *Seigneur des Conardins* from 1724-92. A very elegant wine. Aromatic, floral nose with toasty, nutty, vanilla aromas and rich, rounded fruit on the palate. Long, clean finish and will improve further with a little ageing.

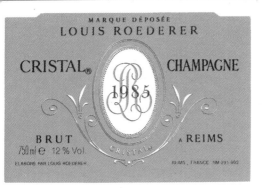

LOUIS ROEDERER

21 Blvd Lundy, 51053 Reims
Tel: 26 40 42 11

History. The House was founded in 1776 by a M. Dubois who was succeeded by a M. Schreider. More than fifty years later, in 1827, the young Louis Roederer joined the company. He was from Alsace, the nephew of M. Schreider, and when his uncle died in 1833, Louis Roederer became owner of the company and gave it his name.

The fame of Louis Roederer champagne quickly spread and by 1870 Russia was the major market. Annual production topped 2.5 million bottles as export markets expanded throughout Europe and North America.

Louis Roederer died in 1870 and was succeeded by his son, also called Louis, who was a great admirer of the arts and literature. He owned one of the finest libraries in France.

The champagne was such a favourite of Tsar Alexander I that he asked Maison Louis Roederer to set aside every year the very best of their wines. Arrangements were then made for the Tsar's Court Cellarmaster to visit Reims once a year, to taste and approve the selection from the various casks. In 1876 the Tsar decided that he wanted a very special champagne for the exclusive use of his Court, and so 'Cristal' was created. Today, Cristal is still a legend among champagnes, and sought after by champagne-lovers worldwide.

Louis died in 1880 and was succeeded by his sister Léonie Olry-Roederer, and then by her son Léon.

The Russian Revolution in 1917 wiped out 80% of the House's business and Louis Roederer had to set about rebuilding its export markets. In 1932 Léon, a keen and famous hunter, died, and Madame Olry-Roederer began her remarkable 42-year reign as the sole director of the company. She rebuilt the company, restored its reputation and increased its export markets, while at all times insisting on quality before quantity.

The House of Louis Roederer is today controlled by members of the Rouzaud family. The president is Mme Claude Rouzaud, daughter of the late Mme Olry-Roederer, and her son Jean-Claude Rouzaud is managing director. The House owns 180 hectares of vineyards which provide most of its requirements, and every year about 600 people arrive from northern France to hand pick the grapes. The pickers are all fed and housed in one of the seven vineyard properties – three press houses and four pickers' sheds.

The grapes are transported by tractors in fifty-kilogram baskets to the pressing houses and the first fermentation begins in the Roederer cellars in Reims on the second day of the harvest. Blending of the various still wines takes place the following spring, with the process of balancing the *cuvée* a closely-guarded family secret. Roederer has the finest reserve cellar of any of the champagne Houses – the main reason for the remarkable consistency and high quality of all their wines, even the non-vintage ones.

Champagne Louis Roederer has invested overseas in recent years – in Anderson Valley, California; in Hemmeskerk Wines, Tasmania; and Adriano Ramos-Pinto Port in Portugal.

Visiting:	By appointment only.
Vineyards:	180 ha – 55 ha PN Montagne de Reims, 50 ha PN Vallée de la Marne, 75 ha Ch Côtes des Blancs.
Annual Prod:	2.6 million bottles.
Exports:	70%.
House Style:	Rich, rounded, opulent wines. Full-bodied and complex. Biscuity, honeyed, and very, very classy.

Grand Vin Sec (66% PN, 34% Ch)
Labelled 'Rich' for the UK market, and blended from the
harvests of five different years including four years of
vintage wine. Fine but vigorous *mousse*, honeyed, but
well-balanced and not overly sweet. Good structure and
long, firm finish.

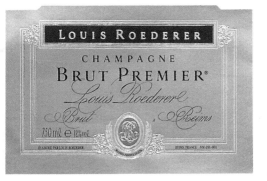

NV Brut Premier (66% PN, 34% Ch)
Contains 8 – 15% reserve wines matured in oak casks for
at least five years, which gives great complexity and
roundness. Fine, lively *mousse,* big, rich nose with gentle
appley, yeasty aromas. Good firm *pinot* fruit on the palate
balanced by *chardonnay* freshness and elegance. Very
well-structured with a long finish.

NV Rosé Brut (70% PN, 30% Ch)
Very ripe bunches of *pinot noir* are left in contact with
the must for up to forty-eight hours to produce a pale
salmon-pink colour, and rich red fruit aromas on the nose.
The wine is aged for three and a half years which gives it
greater depth of berry fruit and complexity. Rich, almost
honeyed, with a long finish. Big enough to match many
dishes and a number of cheeses.

Vintage Brut 1985 (66% PN, 34% Ch)
Produced only in the very best years and aged for five
years. Straw-gold in colour, with a fine, vigorous *mousse.*
It is full bodied with good acidity, depth and complexity,
all the ingredients necessary to produce wines of good
longevity. The style always reflects the characteristics of
the particular vintage.

Vintage Blanc de Blancs Brut 1985 (11% Ch)
Blended from several different *crus* from the Côtes des
Blancs and always a vintage wine. Straw-coloured with a

very fine, delicate *mousse*. It has a dry, steely, elgvant nose, and is light and delicate on the palate with a long, lingering finish. It ages well.

Cristal Vintage Brut 1985 (50-60% PN, 40-50% Ch)
Produced from the finest *cuvées* pressed from the best grapes from their own 100% classification vineyards. Aged for five years, the wine has a brilliant golden colour, and a delicate but persistent *mousse*. It has a fresh, crisp, appley nose with complex toasty, yeasty aromas. Light and elegant on the palate, but with great depth and complexity. A long, strong finish and a wine of great longevity.

RUINART

4 Rue des Crayères, 51100 Reims
Tel: 26 85 40 29

History. Ruinart has the distinction of being the oldest champagne House, having been founded in 1729 by Nicolas Ruinart. He was the first wine merchant credited with selling the sparkling wine, although many others had been selling still wines for generations before. Nicolas was the nephew of Dom Thierry Ruinart, a Benedictine monk who worked with Dom Pérignon, and it was from him that he learnt about champagne.

By the early part of the nineteenth century, Ruinart had a worldwide reputation. It was favoured by the Russian Imperial Court and was one of the best-selling champagnes in the United States.

Ruinart's son Claude joined the firm in 1764, and his eldest son Irénee, apart from selling the wine to many of the Royal Courts and Europe, was a prominent Champagne politican and a mayor of Epernay. Irénee's son Edmond was responsible for the House's success it the United States.

André Ruinart, who took over in 1888, sponsored the first cross-Channel air race. He conducted the firm's affairs from one of the cellars deep underground after the offices had been destroyed by shelling during the Battle of the Marne during World War I. The firm's major expansion took place in the 1950s, and in 1962 it became part of the giant Moët-Hennessy group.

Visiting:	Open weekdays. Weekends by appointment.
Vineyards:	15 ha at Sillery (*chardonnay*) and Brimont.
Annual Prod:	1.4 million bottles.
Exports:	65-70%.
House Style:	Very light, elegant, flowery wines, often with the tell-tale Ruinart citrus touch. Always good value.

NV 'R' de Ruinart (70% PN/PM, 30% Ch)
Very youthful and fresh, with grassy, floral aromas on the nose and ripe, mouth-filling fruit. Good balance and depth, and a long finish.

Vintage 'R' de Ruinart (70% PN/PM, 30% Ch)
A very elegant wine with complex nose full of floral,
fruity, yeasty and vanilla aromas. A surprising richness
on the palate. Rounded balanced fruit and a long, clean,
crisp finish.

Vintage Dom Ruinart Rosé Brut (50% Ch, 50% PN)
Very delicate, light pink colour with fine, creamy,
persistent *mousse*. Very soft and creamy nose with rich,
ripe rounded red fruit on the palate. A long, lingering,
clean finish.

Vintage Dom Ruinart Brut Blanc de Blancs (100% Ch)
The prestige *cuvée* and deservedly so. Gloriously deep
golden colour and a very fine, persistent *mousse*. Very
attractive, complex nose of fruity, floral aromas and a hint
of its maturity. Soft, rounded fruit on the palate which
continues throughout to the long, very clean finish.

LOUIS DE SACY

6 Rue de Verzenay, 51380 Verzy
Tel: 26 97 91 13

History. The Sacy family have owned vineyards in
Champagne for at least 350 years. In 1633 Barthelémy Sacy
owned a vineyard at Le Champ Saint-Rémi, near Verzy, in
the heart of the Montagne de Reims.Since then the family
has always lived in Verzy and today André Sacy and his son
Alain cultivate thirty hectares of vines on the famous chalk
soil which gives Champagne its delicacy and brightness.

In recent years the family has made a major investment in
redeveloping and modernising the production facility. It is
proud of its ability to make wines of the highest quality,
using modern techniques while still maintaining traditional
values and skills that have been passed down from
generation to generation.

The hillside winery, about twenty kilometres from Reims,
is within the *grand cru* region of Montagne de Reims, and
the wines of Verzy all have a 100% classification. The
winery uses stainless steel tanks and a grape press which
utilises the latest computer controlled equipment. André and
Alain select the individual wines for each *cuvée*.

Visiting:	None.
Vineyards:	30 ha.
Annual Prod:	300,000 bottles.
Exports:	20%.
House Style:	Traditional, well-made, elegant wines with good balance and depth.

NV Brut (50% N, 40% Ch, 10% PM)
A big nose full of fruity, spicy, herby aromas and touches
of citrus. Big and full-bodied in the mouth, but well-
balanced with a long, lingering finish.

NV Brut Rosé (50% PN, 40% Ch, 10% PM)
Attractive salmon colour and a fine, persistent *mousse.*
Aromas of soft strawberries and a touch of tobacco. Very
attractive on the palate with good fruit. Well-balanced,
and with depth and a very long finish.

Vintage Brut (50% PN, 40% Ch, 10% PM)
Aged for at least five years.

SALON

Le Mesnil-sur-Oger, 51190 Avize
Tel: 26 50 33 69

History. The House was founded by Eugène-Aimé Salon in 1914, more of a hobby to start with. He was born in Champagne in 1867 and had a mixed career as a teacher, a furrier in Paris, and then a politician, before he bought a five-hectare vineyard at le Mesnil-sur-Oger, not far from where he was born. His ambition was to produce the finest-quality champagne from a single vineyard and a single variety – *chardonnay,* but only in the most exceptional years.

The results were stunning, and to increase production he expanded his own vineyard area and bought in only the best grapes from his neighbours. In the 1920s Salon was Maxim's House Champagne. Since its founder's death in 1943, the House has had a number of owners and is now part of the Laurent-Perrier stable.

Today grapes for production are chosen exclusively from the twenty 100%-rated vineyards of the *grand cru* village, and only when the *chef de cave* considers the quality as near perfection as possible, is a vintage declared. There is no malolactic fermentation. Over the past eighty years, Salon have declared only twenty-eight Vintages, the most recent being 1982. The House is a *grande marque.*

Visiting:	None.
Vineyards:	1 ha but grapes bought form a further 10 ha.
Annual Prod:	50-60,000 bottles.
Exports:	80%.
House Style:	Rich, fresh and vibrant wines with great intensity and depth of fruit. Young Salon wines are characterised by their pale golden colour.

Vintage Cuvée 'S', Blanc de Blancs 1979 (100% Ch)
A pale colour with very delicate *mousse* of tiny, persistent bubbles. Fresh and herbacious on the nose with nutty, vanilla and oak aromas. Rich, mouth-filling fruit on the palate, with great depth, balance and complexity. Long, clean, crisp finish.

Vintage Cuvée 'S', Blanc de Blancs 1982 (100% Ch)
Pale golden in colour with very fine, persistent *mousse*.
Very fresh, floral nose with biscuity, nutty, soft fruit
aromas. Still youthful on the palate but with great
concentration of fruit that carries through to the very
long, clean finish. A wine that will become even more
delicious with further ageing.

TAITTINGER

9 Place Saint-Nicaise, 51100 Reims
Tel: 26 85 45 35

History. The House can trace its roots back to 1734 when it was founded by Jacques Fourneaux, son of a Rilly-la-Montagne vineyard owner. It was one of the first of the champagne Houses and it was Jérome Fourneaux who blended the Veuve Clicquot wines for several years after Nicole-Barbe Clicquot was widowed in 1805.

The House was acquired by Pierre Taittinger in 1930 and the name eventually changed simply to Taittinger. Its dramatic growth all stems from then. The vineyard holding was extended and the magnificent Château de la Marguetterie in Pierry was acquired. It was here that the Benedictine monk, Brother Oudart, at the end of the seventeenth century, discovered some of the secrets of champagne production.

Today Taittinger is very proud of its heritage and the fact that it is one of few family-controlled Houses. More than 100,000 people visit the Taittinger cellars every year where 15 million bottles are stored.

The cellars were originally excavated by the Romans, then enlarged by Benedictine monks in the thirteenth century for the storage of wine produced by the abbey of Saint-Nicaise. Taittinger also owns the House of the Counts of Champagne in Reims. It was Thibaud IV, the most famous Count of Champagne, who brought the *chardonnay* vine back from his Crusades in the Middle East.

Taittinger is a *grande marque* House now run by Claude Taittinger.

Visiting:	Open daily 1 March – 31 October, 9.30 am-1 pm. 1 November – 28 February Monday-Friday only.
Vineyards:	250 ha (50% PN, 30% Ch, 20% PM).
Annual Prod:	Over 4 million bottles.
Exports:	67% to 120 countries.
House Style:	A large proportion of *chardonnay* grapes are traditionally used to impart finesse and delicacy, and to produce the distinctive and very attractive Taittingen flowery nose. All the wines have elegance, depth and great longevity.

SCEAU DE THIBAUD IV   COMTE DE CHAMPAGNE

CHAMPAGNE

TAITTINGER

Ancienne Maison Fourneaux Forest et Succ

FONDÉE   *Reims*   EN 1734

FRANCE

BRUT   RÉSERVE

ÉLABORÉ PAR TAITTINGER, REIMS FRANCE

PRODUCE OF FRANCE

NM-162-001

750ml ℮   12% vol.

NV Brut Réserve (60% PN/PM, 40% Ch)
The intensity of the floral nose can vary as can the
maturity of the fruit, but generally they are very dry,
rounded, well-balanced, satisfying wines with long
finishes.

Vintage Brut 1893 (60% PN, 40% Ch)
The vintage is produced only in the best years. A blend of
pinot and *chardonnay,* but using only the juice from the
first pressing of the grapes. A lovely big, rich wine with
great balance. Crisp, fruity and biscuity.

Previous recommended vintages – 1982, 1980, 1979 and
1976.

Comtes de Champagne Blanc de Blancs Brut (100% Ch)
Produced only in exceptional years and made exlusively
from the first pressing of *chardonnay* grapes from the best
vineyards in the Côte des Blancs. Powerful, concentrated
aromas of nuts and fruit, creamy, soft fruit on the palate
and a long finish with traces of honey and apple. A very
classy, very expensive champagne.

Comtes de Champagne Rosé (100% PN)
Produced in the best years from *pinot noir* grapes from
the to vineyards of Bouzy and Ambonnay in the

Montagne de Reims. The intense colour comes from
leaving the skins to ferment with the grape juice for ten
days at the beginning of fermentation. Full of soft, ripe
fruit and with great balance and length. Will further
improve with age.

Taittinger Collection (60% PN, 40% Ch)
In 1983 Claude Taittinger invited the artist Vasarély to
create a bottle decoration fit for a great vintage. His gold
design accompanied the 1978 vintage, and since then
world-famous artists have been commissioned to create
their own designs – the sculptor Arman for the 1981
vintage, the surrealist artist André Masson for the 1982,
and the abstract painter Maria-Elena Vieira for the 1983.
The fifth bottle in the highly prized and very collectable
Collection has been designed by American artist Roy
Lichenstein for the 1985 vintage. Each edition of the
Collection is limited to 100,000 bottles and is a blend of
both *pinot* and *chardonnay* wines from that vintage.
Magnificent wines of great elegance, balance, length and
longevity.

UNION

7 Rue Pasteur, 51190 Avize
Tel: 26 57 94 22

History. A massive organisation founded in 1966, which represents more than 1,000 growers in nine co-operatives, and produces in excess of five million bottles a year, much of which is privately labelled. Marks & Spencer have been a major UK customer for many years.

Visiting:	By appointment weekdays 9-11 am and 2-4 pm.
Vineyards:	Members own 1,000 ha in Côte des Blancs and Montagne de Reims.
Annual Prod:	5 million bottles, of which about 900,000 are sold under the Union label or one of its *marques,* which include Pierre Vaudon, Saint Gall and René Florancy.
Exports:	30% of its own *marque* bottles.
House Style:	Well-made, good-value, lightish wines with freshness and good fruit.

NV Carte Noire Brut (50/55% PN/PM, 30/35% Ch)
Attractive light- to medium-bodied, with fine persistent *mousse* and rich, fruity *pinot* nose. Good fruit on the palate with depth and balance and a long, clean finish.

NV Blanc de Blancs Brut (100% Ch)
Elegant, soft and creamy. Fine, long-lasting *mousse* and attractive flowery, floral nose with hints of toast and vanilla. Good soft rounded fruit on the palate and good balancing acidity. Long finish.

NV Rosé Brut (100% Ch, with red wine from Bouzy and Ambonnay)
Vigorous *mousse* and good, ripe, red fruit aromas on the nose. Fresh, clean fruit on the palate which lingers to the very end. Very drinkable.

Vintage Brut (100% Ch)
Attractive fruity nose with *brioche,* nut, and vanilla aromas, and rich, rounded fruit flavours on the palate. A long, clean, crisp finish.

Cuvée Spéciale Orpale (100% Ch)
A prestige *cuvée* with considerable elegance and class. A generous proportion of reserve wines provides very good depth and balance. A long, lingering, clean finish.

DE VENOGE

30 Avenue de Champagne, 51204 Epernay
Tel: 26 55 01 01

History. The House was founded in 1837 by Henri-Marc de Venoge, a member of a family of Swiss descent. In the mid-nineteenth century De Venoge wines, thanks to Henri-Marc's son Joseph, became the favourites of many of the Royal houses of Europe, and it was because of this up-market clientele that a special clear bottle was developed to best display the wine. The colour of the reusable decanter has changed over the years but not its shape, and it is still used for the House's prestige *Cuvée des Princes*. The House was acquired by the Trouillard Champagne House in the late 1950s and is now run by Thierry Mantoux who took over in 1986 after five years as export director with Charles Heidsieck-Henriot.

Visiting:	By appointment.
Vineyards:	5.5 ha at Aÿ.
Annual Prod:	1.6 million bottles.
Exports:	45-55%.
House Style:	Big, rounded creamy wines with good maturity. Vintages have great longevity.

NV Cordon Bleu Brut (75% PN, 25% Ch)
An easy-to-drink wine with soft, creamy *mousse* and ripe, currant fruit bouquet, with attractive yeasty aromas. Rich, up-front on the palate and lingers on to a long finish.

NV Blanc de Noirs Brut (100% PN)
A fine, persistent *mousse* and an attractive nose full of fruity, floral and yeasty aromas. Well-balanced and elegant on the palate with a good finish.

NV Blanc de Blancs Brut (100% Ch)
Fine, creamy *mousse* and big, rich *chardonnay* fruit nose full of toasty, biscuity aromas. Good, rounded, soft fruit on the palate and a pleasing lingering finish.

NV Rosé Crémant Brut (Ch/PN blend)
Very drinkable. Fine, persistent creamy *mousse* with floral, fruity nose and rich, ripe fruit on the palate. Stylish, with a lingering finish.

Vintage Brut (85-90% PN, 10-15% Ch)
A big, well-aged wine with fine, persistent *mousse* and powerful red fruit nose with toasty, biscuity aromas. Good ripe fruit on the palate with depth and balance. A long finish and will improve further with ageing.

Cuvée des Princes 1982 (100% Ch)
The House prestige *cuvée,* and deservedly so. A wine of great freshness and elegance that will age beautifully. Fine but vigorous *mousse* and a soft, ripe fruit nose packed with toasty, floral aromas. Still youthful on the palate but with great elegance and balance. Will develop and round with keeping.

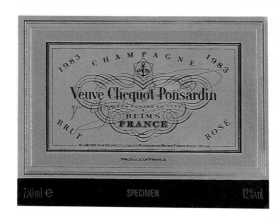

VEUVE CLICQUOT PONSARDIN

12 Rue de Temple, 51100 Reims
Tel: 26 40 25 42

History. One of the oldest and most famous of the champagne Houses. Jean Clicquot was an alderman in Reims in 1722 and welcomed Louis XVI when he entered the city for his coronation. Nicole-Barbe Ponsardin was born during the reign of Louis XVI and in 1798 she married François Clicquot. Public worship was banned during the Directory and the marriage took place in a champagne cellar. In 1803 she gave birth to her only child Clémentine and two years later her husband died. She renamed the company Veuve (widow) Clicquot Ponsardin. An empire was born, and the legend of the Widow, the Grande Dame of champagne, was created.

She was in every sense an innovator. One of the first businesswomen in France, she was the first person to export champagne, and her brand name soon became a favourite throughout the courts of Europe. Today it still carries the warrants of many of Europe's royal houses.

Mme Clicquot invented the riddling table used in *remuage* by adapting a piece of furniture from her own home, and this led to the light, clear champagne we know today. She created the House's distinctive yellow label which is still used after more than 150 years.

She also surrounded herself with able men, one of whom was a M. Bohn, who boosted exports, especially to Britain and Russia. Another was Eduoard Werlé, the business manager who established the company at the forefront of the industry. When she died at the age of eighty-six, the House of Veuve Clicquot Ponsardin had almost become a national institution.

Today tradition still reigns supreme. Grapes are still hand picked and the wines are stored in a network of Roman-excavated chalk cellars which extend for more than twenty-four kilometres. More than 32 million bottles are stored here.

Visiting:	By appointment Monday to Satuday 1 April – 31 October.
Vineyards:	285 ha – 110 ha Ch, 120 ha PN, 54 ha PM – all in the finest *crus* of Champagne. The *pinot noir* comes from Ambonnay, Bouzy, Verzy and Verzenay in the Montagne de Reims; the *chardonnay* from Vertus, Mesnil-sur-Oger, Avize and Cramant on the Côte des Blancs.
Annual Prod:	10 million bottles.
Exports:	84%.
House Style:	Big, rich, classy, mature wines.

NV Brut 'Yellow Label' (56% PN, 28% Ch, 16% PM)
Depending on the *cuvée,* the wines of a single harvest are blended with 25-35% of reserve wines. A brilliant colour with straw-yellow tints. Fine and vigorous *mousse* with a complex fruit and floral nose. Lively, rich, fresh fruit flavours on the palate and a long, lingering finish.

NV Demi-Sec (55% PN, 30% Ch, 15% PM)
An elegant wine with very delicate *mousse,* and attractive balance of sweetness and gently aggressive citrus fruit flavours. Well balanced with a soft, rounded finish.

Vintage Réserve Brut 1983 (33% Ch, 16% PM)
Depending on the *cuvée,* the wines of a single harvest are blended with 25-35% of reserve wines. A brilliant colour with straw-yellow tints. Fine and vigorous *mousse* with a

complex fruit and floral nose. Lively, rich, fresh fruit flavours on the palate and a long, lingering finish.

Vintage Réserve Brut 1983 (33% Ch, 62% PN, 5% PM) A strong, vigorous *mousse* and very elegant *chardonnay* nose with complex floral aromas. A big, rounded wine on the palate with good *pinot* fruit. Very well balanced and a long, long finish.

Previous vintages, all highly recommended – 1982, 1979, 1976 and 1975.

Vintage Rosé Réserve Brut 1983 (66% PN, 34% Ch, with about 15% red Bouzy wine made by traditional vinification in vats with immersed cap and a minimum of six years' ageing)
A lovely salmon-coloured wine with attractive soft, rich fruit and wild strawberry aromas. Surprisingly big on the palate, firm and fruity, with great balance and a long, elegant, lingering finish. The taste of strawberries and red currants clings on to the last.

La Grande Dame Brut 1985 (34% Ch, 66% PN)
A big wine with very fine, persistent and vigorous *mousse*. Very attractive bouquet full of complex floral aromas. Big, fruity and full-bodied on the palate with a long, long finish.

VILMART

4 Rue de la Republique, 51500 Rilly-la-Montagne
Tel: 26 48 40 01

History. The House was founded in 1890 and is run
today by M. and Mme Champs and their son Laurent.
Mme Champs is the great-granddaughter of the founder.

Together with Krug, it is the only House to use only
oak for fermenting and maturing the young wine although
they use much larger barrels than Krug. They own eleven
hectares of *premier cru* vineyards in Rilly. Their
philosophy is to produce grapes in entirely natural
surroundings, using no herbicides or pesticides, and only
organic fertilizers. Vintages are made only in exceptional
years, and are highly sought-after, as they are produced
only in small quantities.

Visiting:	By appointment.
Vineyards:	11 ha in Rilly (50% Ch, 30% PN, 20% PM).
Annual Prod:	80,000 bottles.
Exports:	15-20%.
House Style:	Wines of great class and maturity. Rich, full-bodied and great value.

NV Rubis Brut (blend n/a)
A rosé produced traditionally by allowing the skins to
colour the juice, and then ageing for ten months in oak.
Orangey-pink in colour, with fine, gentle *mousse* and an
attractive, clean nose with hint of richness. It is rich and
vibrant on the palate with good balance and a very long,
almost sweet finish.

NV Cuvée Cellier (50% Ch, 50% PN)
Deep golden colour and fine, even *mousse* with a very
clean nose. Rich and ripe with mouth-filling fruit and
great elegance. A very good finish.

NV Grand Cellier (75% Ch, 25% PN)
A mellow, golden colour, with complex, subtle bouquet
with hints of toffee, oak and toasty *chardonnay*. Full,
rich, strong finish. It will improve even further with
ageing.

NV Grand Cellier d'Or (75% Ch, 25% PN)
A *tête de cuvée* made from a blend of three different
vintages, the youngest being seven years old. It spends an
initial eight months in oak. Fine, creamy *mousse* and deep
colour. Big, powerful bouquet full of fruity, toasty, oaken
aromas. Long and mouth-filling with rich, concentrated
fruit. Full-bodied with a big finish. Will improve further.

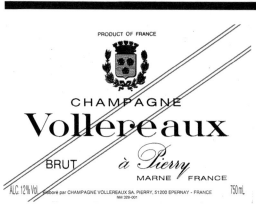

VOLLEREAUX

48 Rue Léon Bourgeois, 51200 Pierry
Tel: 26 54 03 05

History. The House was founded in 1933 and has traditionally concentrated on the French market. The present owner, Pierre Vollereaux, has been responsible for developing exports.

Visiting:	Open Monday to Saturday by appointment.
Vineyards:	40 ha.
Annual Prod:	350-400,000 bottles.
Exports:	15%.
House Style:	Elegant, attractive wines with good balance of fruit and acidity.

NV Brut (33% PN, 33% PM, 33% Ch)
An elegant wine with good balance of fruit and acidity. A fine *mousse*. Good, ripe red fruit on the nose, with rich fruit and crisp acidity balancing on the palate. A good steady finish.

NV Demi-Sec Carte Blanche (33% PN, 33% PM, 33% Ch)
Good fruit and acidity help balance the sweetness. A rich lingering, honeyed finish.

NV Blanc de Blancs Brut (100% Ch)
Creamy and soft, with attractive nose full of soft fruit,
nutty and toasty aromas. Fresh, full fruit flavours on the
palate with a long, lingering finish.

NV Rosé Brut (100% PN)
An attractive *rosé* with creamy red fruit on the nose and
clean, crisp ripe fruit on the palate. Easy-drinking with
good long finish.

Vintage Brut 1983 (80% Ch, 20% PN)
An elegant wine with fine, persistent *mousse* and fruity,
toasty, vanilla aromas on the palate. Good balance and
depth on the palate and a firm finish.

VRANKEN LAFITTE

La Pavé, 51130 Vertus
Tel: 26 52 23 54

History. Vranken Lafitte was established in 1976 by Paul
François Vranken, a Belgian, and with annual production
of more than 3.15 million bottles, it is now one of the
leading champagne Houses. It is unusual in that the
company runs as three separate, autonomous units –
Champagne Demoiselle in Epernay, Champagne Charles
Lafitte in Vertus, and Champagne Sacotte in Congy. Its
produce is sold under a wide variety of labels but its
reputation has been built on the remarkable success of
Champagne Charles Lafitte.

Although still predominantly a Champagne House, the
firm has expanded into Portugal and Spain. It now
controls a 260-hectare Port estate in the Douro Valley.
The vineyards were acquired in 1986, the winery has
been completely modernised, and the wines are shipped
directly from the estate. In association with a Spanish
company, they also manage a 110-hectare estate
producing Cava wines in the High Penedes.

As far as the champagnes are concerned, Champagne
Demoiselle was launched in 1986 and annual sales now
exceed 400,000 bottles. The wine is stored in magnificent
cellars under the Avenue de Champagne, and traditional
methods of wine-making are still used. It is possible to
dine at the cellars. Charles Lafitte was launched in 1983
and sales now top 1.5 million bottles a year.

Visiting:	Weekdays at Champagne Demoiselle (Avenue de Champagne).
Vineyards:	43 ha.
Annual Prod:	3.15 million bottles.
Exports:	15-20%.
House Style:	Elegant, light, fruity, approachable wines. Good value for money.

NV Demoiselle Brut (60% Ch, 40% PN)
A blend of *chardonnay* from *premier cru* and *grand cru*
villages. The paleness in the colour reflects the
predominance of *chardonnay*. A fine, vigorous *mousse*
and big, rich aromatic nose full of *chardonnay* aromas –

creamy, toasty, nutty and appley. It is fresh and light on the palate with good balance and a long finish.

NV Sacotte Brut (20% Ch, 50% PN, 30% PM)
A very pale straw colour with a fine but vigorous *mousse*. Fresh, fruity bouquet with aromas of strawberries and other berry fruits. Big, rich fruit on the palate with a very strong finish.

NV Charles Lafitte Brut (40% Ch, 30% PN, 30% PM)
Soft nose full of fresh fruit and floral aromas, and light and fresh on the palate. Youthful but good *pinot meunier* fruit coming through. Well balanced with a long finish.

Charles Lafitte 'Orgueil de France' Brut (100% Ch)
Produced only from *chardonnay* from *grand cru* vineyards. Pale in colour but with a full, rich nose. Aromas of citrus and hazelnut and hedgerow flowers. A firm wine on the palate, full and round, with pleasing acidity and a long finish.

NV Charles Lafitte Tête de Cuvée Brut (60% Ch, 30% PN, 10% PM)
Golden yellow in colour wtih soft, creamy nose, lots of quince and currant aromas. Elegant, light and rounded on the palate with a long, firm finish.

NV Bruitissime Brut (20% Ch, 40% PN, 40% PM)
Very pale with gold tints. Ripe fruit nose with hints of peaches, and fresh and lively on the palate. Good, rich and fruity but light and well-balanced, with a long finish.

THE GASTRONOMY OF CHAMPAGNE

For centuries they have been eating well in Champagne. There are the *andouillettes* of Troyes, which is also famous for its *charcuteries* and stuffed tongues. There are *boudins*, brawn and ham, from Reims and the neighbouring Ardennes, which also produces a fine array of game. Thrushes are a local delicacy, and there are excellent local meats and vegetables. The cooking in the region can range from the very rich, to the more humble but equally enjoyable fare such as dandelion salad. Champagne also enjoys its desserts, such as meringues, macaroons and honeyed gingerbreads, and there is a marvellous selection of cheeses.

Champagne is, of course, used in cooking chicken, snails and meat, and for poaching the local freshwater fish, but the adventurous traveller who gets off the beaten track and away from the tourist circuit will be rewarded by finding traditional cuisine.

Pork and *charcuterie* is, as already mentioned, a speciality of the region. Perhaps the most famous dish is *pieds de porc à la Ste Ménéhould,* which is pigs' trotters slowly grilled and poached until the bones are so soft that they can be eaten. There is *jambon en croûte,* which is ham cooked in a rich pastry, and smoked hams such as those from the Ardennes. *Andouilles* are made from a pig's large intestine stuffed with strips of chitterlings and tripe. *Andouillette* is a smaller version, but is usually grilled and served hot with a hot mustard sauce. *Andoiullettes de mouton* are a speciality of Troyes; they are made from mutton and heavily spiced.

Other sausages include *boudin noir,* which, like English black pudding, is made from blood, and *boudin blanc,* often made with chicken. *Boudin Ste Ménéhould* is made from rabbit, which is the basis of many other local dishes.

Both rabbit *(lapin)* and hare *(lièvre)* are to be found on menus. *Lapin Valenciennes* is rabbit stewed with prunes and raisins, with either wine or beer. *Civet de lièvre* is the French equivalent of jugged hare, and both rabbit and hare are used to produce delicious pâtés.

Other game brought in from the Ardennes includes wild boar and deer. Boar is *sanglier,* and *marcassin ardennaise* is young boar (under a year old) roasted in red wine sauce with bacon, celeriac and juniper berries.

Other meat dishes are *langue de Valenciennes Lucullus* (smoked tongue with foie gras), *hochepot* (a meat and vegetable stew), *carbonnade flamande* (beef braised in beer with onions) and *potée champenoise*, which is a very filling stew of bacon, ham, sausage and cabbage.

Pigeons and thrushes which have gorged themselves on the grapes during the summer are also offered on menus. Often they come *en croûte*, but thrushes *(grives)* are also roasted and served whole on a bed of vine leaves. Other birds on the menu are likely to be quail *(caille)*, pigeon and woodcock *(bécasse)*. All make lovely pâtés.

In addition to pâtés there are *terrines* made from duck, rabbit, veal and chicken. Potje flesh or *potie vleesch*, although a Flanders dish, is served here and is a *terrine* of veal, chicken and rabbit. Quenelles, too, are popular and use either meat or fish. *Quenelles de brochet* are poached pike in a creamy sauce, *Pain à la reine* is fish *mousse*, which also includes pike, as does *cervelat de brochet*, a sort of pike sausage which is very light.

Other fish on the menu include: *carpe* (carp), *truite* (trout), *anguilles* (eels) and *barcillon* (barbel). The last is often served in champagne. *Anguille au vert* is eel served in a herb and wine sauce. *Saterelles* may appear on menus instead of the more usual *crevettes* (both are shrimps).

There are good local snails *(escargots)* served either in champagne sauce or with garlic butter. *Chou rouge à la flamande* is red cabbage stewed in vinegar with sugar and apples, and *ficelle picarde* is another succulent import – a ham and mushroom pancake with a white, buttery sauce.

Flamiche is pumpkin or leek tart with cream, and *gougère* is a cheese-flavoured choux pastry ring, served cold. Another regional speciality is *salade de pissenlits au lard*, made from fresh dandelion leaves cooked in pork fat with vinegar, and served wth diced bacon *(lardons)* and french bread or potatoes.

Champagne also has more than its fair share of desserts and confectionery. There are *anglois* (plum tart), *galopin* (bread pancakes sprinkled with sugar), and *gaufres* (waffles). There are the delicate *biscuits de Reims* which you can dunk in a glass of champagne, and other macaroons. *Pain d'épices* is spiced gingerbread, often with honey, while *kokeboterom* comes originally from

Flanders – it is the Dutch word for cake – and is a small raisin bun. You may also see either *talibur* or *rabote* on the menu. This is a whole apple cooked in a pastry case, a speciality of Champagne.

Because Champagne is surrounded by agricultural land, many of the cheeses it sells are really from outside the region, but it does have some of its own, and you are likely to be offered both the local and the outside varieties in a restaurant.

Barbey is a speciality Champenois cheese, also known as *fromage de Troyes* or *Troyen cendré* because it comes from the village of Barbéry near Troyes. It is a soft cheese cured in wood ashes and shaped into rounds. It is made from cows' milk. *Chaource* is a very delicate cows' milk cheese with a fruity taste. It is soft and creamy, shaped into rounds, and is a speciality of the region, with its own *appellation*.

Langres is a strong Champagne cheese. It is made from cows' milk by small dairies and shaped to cones. It is a strong-smelling cheese but not strong to the taste. *Ervy-le-Châtel,* made around the town of the same name in Champagne, is a strong cows'-milk cheese, cone-shaped and with a mushroom smell. *Coulommiers* is really from the Ile-de-France, but it is widely available in Champagne and some dairies have started to produce it. It is quite strong-smelling but has a *brie* taste. *Caprice des dieux* is a Champagne cheese, factory-made, pasteurised and very creamy. *Chaumont* too is a Champagne speciality, a strong-smelling, spicy cheese. *Carré de l'est* comes from both Champagne and Lorraine, and is a white creamy cheese similar to *camembert.*

GLOSSARY

AC/AOC	Appellation Contrôlée/Appellation d'Origine Contrôlée
assemblage	the blending of base wines to produce a *cuvée*
atmosphère	A measure of pressure, 1 atmosphere = 15 pounds per square inch
blanc de blancs	wines made from only white grapes
blanc de noirs	wines made from only red grapes
BOB	Buyer's Own Brand
brut	dry
brut absolut	(also brut intégral, brut non-dosage) bone dry
cave	an underground cellar
cellier	an above ground cellar
chai	wine store-house
chardonnay	the only white grape variety permitted in Champagne
CM	Coopérative de Manipulation (made by a co-operative)
CIVC	Comité Interprofessionnel du Vin de Champagne
crémant	slightly less pressure and with smaller bubbles
cru	a grape-producing village or commune
cuve	an oak barrel or vat, or tank
cuvée	the blend of wines used in the finished product
cuvée de prestige	the House's top-of-the-range wine
dégorgement	the removal of sediment from the neck of the bottle after *remuage*
demi sec	sweet
dosage	sugar added to champagne after dégorgement for sweetness prior to sale
doux	very sweet, to be drunk with dessert (same as rich)
echelle des crus	the classificatin used to judge the quality of grapes produced by different vineyards or crus.
grand cru	villages with a 100% échelle rating
grande marque	Used by Houses belonging to the Syndicat de Grandes Marques de Champagne.
gyrasol	computer-controlled rotating pallets that have largely taken over the work of *remuage*
lies	the lees, or sediment in the bottom of tank or vat after fermentation

sur lie	to keep the wine in contact with the lees
MA, Marque d'Acheteur	Buyer's Own Brand
malolactic fermentation	used to soften wines or speed up maturation
marque	a brand name
méthode champenoise	the traditional way of producing Champagne. It can only be applied to wines made there.
millésime	the vintage year
mousse	the bubbles
NM, Négociant-Manipulant	champagne House
NV	non-vintage
pinot meunier	one of the only two black grape varieties allowed
pinot noir	the other black grape variety permitted, and superior
premier cru	vineyard villages or communes with an échelle rating of 90 – 99%
RC, Récoltant-Coopérateur	a grower selling champagne produced by a co-operative
RD, récemment dégorgé	kept under ideal conditions and disgorged just prior to release
remuage	the manipulation of the bottle to move the sediment to the neck for *dégorgement*
reserve wines	wines held from previous vintages added for balance and quality
rich	very sweet, to be drunk with dessert (same as *doux*)
RM, Récoltant-Manipulant	a grower producing Champagne from his own grapes
sans année	non-vintage, not dated
sec	slightly sweet
SR, Société de Récoltant	a company created by wine growers who are all members of the same family
tête de cuvée	the first juice from the pressing and the highest quality
vendange	the harvest
vigneron	a vine grower

SOME STATISTICS

Principal world markets (bottles)	1990	% difference over 1989
UK	21,291,532	– 6.58
Germany	14,237,831	+9.93
United States	11,669,222	–14.65
Italy	9,626,094	+5.67
Switzerland	8,599,632	–7.71
Belgium	5,886,197	+0.33
Netherlands	1,652,889	–17.40
Japan	1,509,123	+17.40
Australia	1,231,529	–22.38
Spain	983,956	+3.90
France	147,578,584	–4.54
Total exports	84,787,098	–10.10
Total	232,365,682	–6.64

	1991	% difference over 1990
Germany	14,053,550	–1.29%
UK	14,026,078	–34.12%
United States	10,185,581	–12.7%
Italy	9,042,900	–6.06%
Switzerland	6,931,273	–19,40%
Belgium	5,243,252	–10.9%
Netherlands	1,704,675	+3.13%
Japan	1,426,498	–5.8%
Australia	829,588	–32.64%
Spain	905,130	–8.01%
France	132,500,000	
Total exports	77,500,000	
Total	210,000,000	

	1992	% difference over 1991
UK	14,659,625	+4.5%
Germany	13,609,231	–3.2%
USA	9,997,347	–1.8%
Italy	8,122,650	–10.2%
Switzerland	6,425,772	–7.3%
Belgium	5,765,832	+9.9%
Netherlands	1,462,758	–14.2%
Spain	1,023,401	+13.0%
Japan	1,021,302	–28.4%
Australia	881,739	+6.3%
France	140,770,972	
Total Exports	73,438,289	
Total	214,209,261	

Exports 1970-1992	United Kingdom	United States
1970	6,317,143	4,509,626
1971	7,374,485	3,748,766
1972	8,155,210	4,329,534
1973	10,346,850	3,905,739
1974	4,575,976	2,874,504
1975	3,064,594	2,985,396
1976	5,281,686	4,013,412
1977	7,305,271	4,926,363
1978	8,187,964	7,169,224
1979	9,209,306	7,817,130
1980	8,517,954	7,905,480
1981	7,879,907	7,885,155
1982	7,771,632	7,082,964
1983	10,021,164	9,178,538
1984	11,903,242	12,820,067
1985	15,351,080	14,227,993
1986	16,105,758	14,854,468
1987	19,247,561	15,837,097
1988	20,648,226	14,507,582
1989	22,792,260	13,673,096
1990	21,291,532	11,669,222
1991	14,026,078	10,185,581
1992	14,659,625	9,997,347

Champagne vintages declared since 1900

1900	1928	1953	1973	1983
1904	1929	1955	1974 (only Roederer)	1984
1906	1934	1959*	1975	1985
1911*	1937	1961	1976*	1986
1914*	1941	1962	1977 (only Roederer)	
1915	1943*	1964	1978	
1917	1945*	1966	1979	
1919*	1947	1969	1980	
1921*	1949	1970	1981	
1923	1952	1971	1982	

*Exceptional vintages

CHAMPAGNE HARVESTS
SINCE 1970

1970, 210,585,037 bottle equivalents. A good year.

1971, 81,678,252. A small, irregular crop.

1972, 148,932,760. Cold and wet, not sufficient September sun to ensure full ripening in many vineyards. No vintage wines made.

1973, 202,096,788. A warm spring and summer led to an early harvest which started on 28 September.

1974, 163,216,035. Cold, wet second half of September hindered ripening in some areas.

1975, 168,580,732. September storms meant rotting or damaged grapes had to be removed from the bunches before pressing.

1976, 203,533,289. Ideal early June for flowering. Hot summer. Picking began on 1 September, the earliest since 1893.

1977, 185,660,067. Spring frosts and a damp summer caused mildew and grey rot.

1978, 79,297,401. Very small harvest caused by late flowering but good quality.

1979, 228,581,961. Warm summer produced a good quality, abundant crop.

1980, 113,179,850. Extensive rain reduced quantity, but good quality crop.

1981, 92,246,666. Frost in April, hail in May, cold July and wet September. A difficult year producing a small crop.

1982, 295,199,926. Frost-free winter and spring and long warm summer. Ideal conditions and a record harvest.

1983, 302,033,326. Second record crop in a row after another excellent year.

1984, 198,986,660. Late harvest (8 October) because of late flowering.

1985, 151,891,660. Extreme winter (−30°C) and spring frosts killed 2,000 ha of vines. Perfect September and October partly redeemed the situation. A second picking took place at the end of October in some areas. Yields ranged from virtually nothing in the worst frost-hit areas to more than 10,000 kg per hectare. Quality was exceptionally high.

1986, 259,017,500. Exceptionally fine weather at flowering although heavy rain in August and September did some damage. Quality ranged from good to very good. Unusually high yields up to 14,400 kg per hectare.

1987, 264,404,063. Late harvest after an appalling June. Quality generally good, and high yields at 11,641 kg per hectare.

1988, 224,000,000. Record early flowering (started on 12 June) and picking started on 19 September. Grape quality was excellent but yields down. An average 9,654 kg per hectare.

1989, 275,000,000. "Without precedent in living memory". End-of-April frosts caused considerable damage. Violently fluctuating weather affected flowering, especially of *chardonnay,* but an idyllic summer led to early harvest which started on 4 September. The proportion of tartaric acid was greater than that of malic acid, which is exceptional. The harvest was the seventh largest in the last thirty years.

1990, 287,828,410. Very early flowering in some areas led to early harvest (1 September). The crop was the third largest on record and the fifth successive above-average yield. The average yield was 11,944 kg per hectare. Quality was good to very good.

1991,273,899,781. One-third of Champagne's vineyards, especially in the Aisne and the Aube, were seriously affected by spring frosts which hit yields. Most other areas, however, produced above average crops and the vintage has been describe as 'a Classic year'. The total yield is the fifth largest ever recorded, and the yield per hectare was 11,199 kilos, the ninth largest since 1970.

1992, (equivalent to 280 million bottles). For the first time since 1988 the Champage vineyards escaped damage from late spring frosts and there was a satisfactory flowering in mid-June, despite cooler weather and heavy rainfalls. Yields were higher than average and the harvest started on 14 September in the Côte des Blancs and ended around 10 October. The weather was favourable throughout. The harvest, the equivalent of 280 million bottles was the fourth largest on record but almost one-quarter of the resulting 'must' has been put in reserve to supplement any shortfall in the crop in future years.